SCHOLASTIC

GRADES 6–8

Using Benchmark Papers to Teach Writing With the Traits

Middle School

S0-AGJ-278

RUTH CULHAM

With Linda Brock

New York • Toronto • London • Auckland • Sydney
Mexico City • New Delhi • Hong Kong • Buenos Aires

Teaching *Resources*

Cover design by Brian LaRossa
Interior design by Sarah Morrow

Copyright © 2010 by Ruth Culham
All rights reserved. Published by Scholastic Inc.
Printed in the U.S.A.
ISBN-13: 978-0-545-13840-6
ISBN-10: 0-545-13840-X

2 3 4 5 6 7 8 9 10 11   40   17 16 15 14 13 12 11 10

Contents

Voice

Word Choice

Sentence Fluency

Conventions

* *These papers appear as Interactive PDFs on the CD. All papers are available in PDF format on the CD.*

Introduction

Since the inception of the writing trait model in the mid-1980s, teachers and students have been better able to communicate about what makes a piece of writing work by focusing discussion on the traits: ideas, organization, voice, word choice, sentence fluency, and conventions. Having a common language for talking about and working with student writing has been a powerful breakthrough in the assessment and teaching of writing. And what better way to make the traits concrete than by showing students examples of them in actual writing? Even better, in writing created by students just like themselves?

As teachers have embraced the traits, they have expanded their teaching of writing, moving from simply assigning topics to demonstrating how to make a piece richer in a specific trait. And they have told me—again and again as I travel around the country—how much they need a collection of student work that shows the range of possibilities, from "rudimentary" to "exceptional" in every trait, for the levels at which they teach: grades 6, 7, and 8.

In response to that need, my colleague Linda Brock of Blue Springs, Missouri, and I have collected hundreds of papers over the past several years. We sorted them and selected the exemplars we present here—a rich and thorough collection of papers that represents the range of written work we've found in grades 6, 7, and 8. These models will help students learn to spot the traits, see what successful writers do with each of the traits, and study how they affect the writing as a whole.

This book contains six papers per trait, ranging from high to low in ideas, organization, voice, word choice, sentence fluency, and conventions for a total of 36 exemplars from grades 6–8. Each paper is annotated with a detailed explanation of how it was assessed for the specific trait, using the traits of writing scoring guides on pages 10–15. Additionally, for each paper we offer a conference comment you might share with a writer in your class who is working at the same skill level, complimenting him or her on what is done well and posing a suggestion for revision or editing the piece in that trait.

We've included all the papers on the enclosed CD as PDFs, so you can easily print or project papers to share with your students. The CD also contains twelve interactive whiteboard activities based on the key qualities, so students can explore a high and low paper in each trait in a fun, motivating way. There are suggested activities for them to try with the papers, too, so whether you are leading the lesson or they are working in small groups practicing their writing together, these papers can be a big help.

The traits are a powerful way to dig deeply into writing, to show writers how they are doing and what to try next. In particular they provide us with the language to engage students in revision and editing activities, two cornerstones of the writing process. Having a common language for talking about writing makes the whole process easier for kids and teachers alike by helping them understand how writing works. They will appreciate having the traits as tools in their ever-growing writer's toolbox—tools they can really use because they've seen examples of them in action.

Part I: How to Use the Benchmark Paper Collection

From the beginning, samples of student writing have been central to the clarity and validity of the writing traits model. When the traits emerged in the mid-1980s, teachers gathered samples of student writing and sorted them holistically into piles: high, middle, and low. Those three piles became five as distinctions between papers became more clear: some papers were better than those in the middle, but not quite as good as the ones in the high group, for instance. Finally, a sixth pile was added for those few papers that soared beyond anyone's wildest expectations.

Once the papers were sorted, teachers were given the task of documenting why each paper was placed in a specific pile by asking, "What makes this paper better or worse than those in adjacent stacks?" Answers varied: sometimes the idea was not clear, but the spelling and punctuation were strong. In other papers, the sentences were choppy and the words imprecise, yet the introduction and flow of the text worked well. After much analysis, the lists of writing qualities that teachers noted were grouped and the traits (ideas, organization, voice, word choice, sentence fluency, and conventions) emerged as six elements found in every sample of writing, no matter how successful the writing might have been overall. Eventually, a seventh trait—presentation—was added so teachers had a place to assess the physical appearance of a paper, which is more of a fine-motor and visual skill than the other traits. In this book, however, we focus on the first six traits.

The traits surfaced, were named, and then were defined at different performance levels because teachers closely examined samples of student writing. It's as simple as that. Scoring guides were drafted and used to assess writing in each of the traits. Through this process, an analytic model that pinpointed strengths and revealed weaknesses in each of the six different traits became one of the most valuable tools in the writing teacher's classroom: once teachers could assess writing with accuracy and reliability, what students needed to improve became crystal clear. Although the scoring guides continue to be revised to tighten and clarify their language, the way they are consistently anchored to student writing makes them authentic and powerful tools that will never go out of date. The exemplars in this book show how the traits are typically expressed in the writing of middle school students, and the annotations link directly back to the scoring guides. You can use the papers to hone your own assessment sense and to help students learn more about writing, trait by trait.

Defining the Traits for Middle School Writers

Before students can begin using the traits, they need to know what the traits are. Broken down into seven categories, the traits are straightforward and logical. Here is a simple definition of each:

- *Ideas:* the piece's content—its central message and details that support the message
- *Organization:* the internal structure of the piece—the thread of logic, the pattern of meaning
- *Voice:* the tone and tenor of the piece—the personal stamp of the writer, which is achieved through a strong understanding of purpose and audience
- *Word Choice:* the vocabulary the writer uses to convey meaning and enlighten the reader
- *Sentence Fluency:* the way the words and phrases flow throughout the text— it is the auditory trait; we "read" for it with the ear as much as the eye
- *Conventions:* the mechanical correctness of the piece—correct use of conventions (spelling, capitalization, punctuation, paragraphing, and grammar and usage) guides the reader through the text and makes it easy to follow
- *Presentation:* the physical appearance of the piece—a visually appealing text provides a welcome mat; it invites the reader in

Middle schoolers do not have full control over these critical writing skills yet, but they are well on their way. To make the traits more student-friendly, we've broken each one down into four key qualities, which are teachable and easy to spot in writing samples.

Ideas

- Finding a Topic
- Focusing the Topic
- Developing the Topic
- Using Details

Organization

- Creating the Lead
- Using Sequence Words and Transition Words
- Structuring the Body
- Ending With a Sense of Resolution

Word Choice

- Applying Strong Verbs
- Selecting Striking Words and Phrases
- Using Specific and Accurate Words
- Choosing Words That Deepen Meaning

Sentence Fluency

- Crafting Well-Built Sentences
- Varying Sentence Types
- Capturing Smooth and Rhythmic Flow
- Breaking the "Rules" to Create Fluency

Voice	*Conventions*
• Establishing a Tone	• Checking Spelling
• Conveying the Purpose	• Punctuating Effectively and Paragraphing Accurately
• Creating a Connection to the Audience	• Capitalizing Correctly
• Taking Risks to Create Voice	• Applying Grammar and Usage

The key qualities allow us to get inside the trait and learn about its different components. Embedding the key qualities into the scoring guide is a new format we hope you'll appreciate. You can use them to assess, but you can also use them to teach. Trying to teach "ideas," for instance, is just too big. But you can teach students how to find an idea and how to focus it. These are teachable skills that the papers in this collection are intended to help you show to students as they learn about each trait and apply this knowledge to their writing.

Noticing what student writers do, naming it, and showing them the next step to take are essential to their success. Good writing happens over time and with lots of practice and lots of support. The traits give you the language and structure to move students forward, step by step, as they develop from beginning writers to writers with strong and consistently good writing skills.

Understanding and Using the Middle School Scoring Guide

The trait scoring guides on pages 10–15 allow you to assess student writing and provide feedback that students can use to make their current and future work stronger. Scores range from 1 to 6 in each of the traits and fall into one of three zones: high, middle, or low. For example, if a student writes the roughest of drafts, showing little control and skill in the trait for which you're assessing, he or she would receive a score of 1, Rudimentary, in the low zone. But if his or her piece shows especially strong control and skill in the trait, he or she would receive a score of 6, Exceptional, in the high zone.

This book provides an exemplar for each point on the scale for each trait along with an explanation of the score and a suggested comment to share with the student during a conference. On the CD, we've also included a copy of the student-friendly guide for middle school writers to use for self-assessment and for use at conferences where you and your students will have discussions about each trait and set goals for the next steps they should take to improve their writing.

Scoring Guide: Ideas

The piece's content—its central message and details that support that message

6 **HIGH** **EXCEPTIONAL**

A. **Finding a Topic:** The writer offers a clear, central theme or a simple, original story line that is memorable.

B. **Focusing the Topic:** The writer narrows the theme or story line to create a piece that is clear, tight, and manageable.

C. **Developing the Topic:** The writer provides enough critical evidence to support the theme and shows insight on the topic. Or he or she tells the story in a fresh way through an original, unpredictable plot.

D. **Using Details:** The writer offers credible, accurate details that create pictures in the reader's mind, from the beginning of the piece to the end. Those details provide the reader with evidence of the writer's knowledge about and/or experience with the topic.

5 **STRONG**

4 **MIDDLE** **REFINING**

A. **Finding a Topic:** The writer offers a recognizable but broad theme or story line. He or she stays on topic, but in a predictable way.

B. **Focusing the Topic:** The writer needs to crystallize his or her topic around the central theme or story line. He or she does not focus on a specific aspect of the topic.

C. **Developing the Topic:** The writer draws on personal knowledge and experience, but does not offer a unique perspective. He or she does not probe deeply, but instead gives the reader only a glimpse at aspects of the topic.

D. **Using Details:** The writer offers details, but they do not always hit the mark because they are inaccurate or irrelevant. He or she does not create a picture in the reader's mind because key questions about the central theme or story line have not been addressed.

3 **DEVELOPING**

2 **LOW** **EMERGING**

A. **Finding a Topic:** The writer has not settled on a topic and, therefore, may offer only a series of unfocused, repetitious, and/or random thoughts.

B. **Focusing the Topic:** The writer has not narrowed his or her topic in a meaningful way. It's hard to tell what the writer thinks is important since he or she devotes equal importance to each piece of information.

C. **Developing the Topic:** The writer has created a piece that is so short, the reader cannot fully understand or appreciate what he or she wants to say. He or she may have simply restated an assigned topic or responded to a prompt, without devoting much thought or effort to it.

D. **Using Details:** The writer has clearly devoted little attention to details. The writing contains limited or completely inaccurate information. After reading the piece, the reader is left with many unanswered questions.

1 **RUDIMENTARY**

Using Benchmark Papers to Teach Writing With the Traits: Middle School © 2010 by Ruth Culham, Scholastic Teaching Resources

Scoring Guide: Organization

The internal structure of the piece—the thread of logic, the pattern of meaning

6 EXCEPTIONAL

A. **Creating the Lead:** The writer grabs the reader's attention from the start and leads him or her into the piece naturally. He or she entices the reader, providing a tantalizing glimpse of what is to come.

B. **Using Sequence Words and Transition Words:** The writer includes a variety of carefully selected sequence words (such as *later*, *then*, and *meanwhile*) and transition words (such as *however*, *also*, and *clearly*), which are placed wisely to guide the reader through the piece by showing how ideas progress, relate, and/or diverge.

C. **Structuring the Body:** The writer creates a piece that is easy to follow by fitting details together logically. He or she slows down to spotlight important points or events, and speeds up when he or she needs to move the reader along.

D. **Ending With a Sense of Resolution:** The writer sums up his or her thinking in a natural, thoughtful, and convincing way. He or she anticipates and answers any lingering questions the reader may have, providing a strong sense of closure.

5 STRONG

4 REFINING

A. **Creating the Lead:** The writer presents an introduction, although it may not be original or thought-provoking. Instead, it may be a simple restatement of the topic and, therefore, does not create a sense of anticipation about what is to come.

B. **Using Sequence Words and Transition Words:** The writer uses sequence words to show the logical order of details, but they feel obvious or canned. The use of transition words is spotty and rarely creates coherence.

C. **Structuring the Body:** The writer sequences events and important points logically, for the most part. However, the reader may wish to move a few things around to create a more sensible flow. He or she may also feel the urge to speed up or slow down for more satisfying pacing.

D. **Ending With a Sense of Resolution:** The writer ends the piece on a familiar note: "Thank you for reading…," "Now you know all about…," or "They lived happily ever after." He or she needs to tie up loose ends to leave the reader with a sense of satisfaction or closure.

3 DEVELOPING

2 EMERGING

A. **Creating the Lead:** The writer does not give the reader any clue about what is to come. The opening point feels as if it was chosen randomly.

B. **Using Sequence Words and Transition Words:** The writer does not provide sequence and/or transition words between sections, or provides words that are so confusing the reader is unable to sort one section from another.

C. **Structuring the Body:** The writer does not show clearly what comes first, next, and last, making it difficult to understand how sections fit together. The writer slows down when he or she should speed up, and speeds up when he or she should slow down.

D. **Ending With a Sense of Resolution:** The writer ends the piece with no conclusion at all—or nothing more than "The End" or something equally bland. There is no sense of resolution, no sense of completion.

1 RUDIMENTARY

Scoring Guide: Voice

The tone and tenor of the piece—the personal stamp of the writer, which is achieved through a strong understanding of purpose and audience

6

HIGH

EXCEPTIONAL

A. **Establishing a Tone:** The writer cares about the topic, and it shows. The writing is expressive and compelling. The reader feels the writer's conviction, authority, and integrity.

B. **Conveying the Purpose:** The writer makes clear his or her reason for creating the piece. He or she offers a point of view that is appropriate for the mode (narrative, expository, or persuasive), which compels the reader to read on.

C. **Creating a Connection to the Audience:** The writer speaks in a way that makes the reader want to listen. He or she has considered what the reader needs to know and the best way to convey it by sharing his or her fascination, feelings, and opinions about the topic.

D. **Taking Risks to Create Voice:** The writer expresses ideas in new ways, which makes the piece interesting and original. The writing sounds like the writer because of his or her use of distinctive, just-right words and phrases.

5

STRONG

4

MIDDLE

REFINING

A. **Establishing a Tone:** The writer has established a tone that can be described as "pleasing" or "sincere," but not "passionate" or "compelling." He or she attempts to create a tone that hits the mark, but the overall result feels generic.

B. **Conveying the Purpose:** The writer has chosen a voice for the piece that is not completely clear. There are only a few moments when the reader understands where the writer is coming from and why he or she wrote the piece.

C. **Creating a Connection to the Audience:** The writer keeps the reader at a distance. The connection between reader and writer is tenuous because the writer reveals little about what is important or meaningful about the topic.

D. **Taking Risks to Create Voice:** The writer creates a few moments that catch the reader's attention, but only a few. The piece sounds like anyone could have written it. It lacks the energy, commitment, and conviction that would distinguish it from other pieces on the same topic.

3

DEVELOPING

2

LOW

EMERGING

A. **Establishing a Tone:** The writer has produced a lifeless piece—one that is monotonous, mechanical, repetitious, and/or off-putting to the reader.

B. **Conveying the Purpose:** The writer chose the topic for mysterious reasons. The piece may be filled with random thoughts, technical jargon, or inappropriate vocabulary, making it impossible to discern how the writer feels about the topic.

C. **Creating a Connection to the Audience:** The writer provides no evidence that he or she has considered what the reader might need to know to connect with the topic. Or there is an obvious mismatch between the piece's tone and the intended audience.

D. **Taking Risks to Create Voice:** The writer creates no highs and lows. The piece is flat and lifeless, causing the reader to wonder why he or she wrote it in the first place. The writer's voice does not pop out, even for a moment.

1

RUDIMENTARY

Using Benchmark Papers to Teach Writing With the Traits: Middle School © 2010 by Ruth Culham, Scholastic Teaching Resources

Scoring Guide: Word Choice

The specific vocabulary the writer uses to convey meaning and enlighten the reader

6
HIGH

EXCEPTIONAL

A. **Applying Strong Verbs:** The writer uses many "action words," giving the piece punch and pizzazz. He or she has stretched to find lively verbs that add energy to the piece.

B. **Selecting Striking Words and Phrases:** The writer uses many finely honed words and phrases. His or her creative and effective use of literary techniques such as alliteration, simile, and metaphor makes the piece a pleasure to read.

C. **Using Specific and Accurate Words:** The writer uses words with precision. He or she selects words the reader needs to fully understand the message. The writer chooses nouns, adjectives, adverbs, and so forth that create clarity and bring the topic to life.

D. **Choosing Words That Deepen Meaning:** The writer uses words to capture the reader's imagination and enhance the piece's meaning. There is a deliberate attempt to choose the best word over the first word that comes to mind.

5

STRONG

4
MIDDLE

REFINING

A. **Applying Strong Verbs:** The writer uses the passive voice quite a bit and includes few "action words" to give the piece energy.

B. **Selecting Striking Words and Phrases:** The writer provides little evidence that he or she has stretched for the best words or phrases. He or she may have attempted to use literary techniques, but they are clichés for the most part.

C. **Using Specific and Accurate Words:** The writer presents specific and accurate words, except for those related to sophisticated and/or content-related topics. Technical or irrelevant jargon is off-putting to the reader. The words rarely capture the reader's imagination.

D. **Choosing Words That Deepen Meaning:** The writer fills the piece with unoriginal language rather than language that results from careful revision. The words communicate the basic idea, but they are ordinary and uninspired.

3

DEVELOPING

2
LOW

EMERGING

A. **Applying Strong Verbs:** The writer makes no attempt to select verbs with energy. The passive voice dominates the piece.

B. **Selecting Striking Words and Phrases:** The writer uses words that are repetitive, vague, and/ or unimaginative. Limited meaning comes through because the words are so lifeless.

C. **Using Specific and Accurate Words:** The writer misuses words, making it difficult to understand what he or she is conveying. Or he or she uses words that are so technical, inappropriate, or irrelevant the average reader can hardly understand what he or she is saying.

D. **Choosing Words That Deepen Meaning:** The writer uses many words and phrases that simply do not work. Little meaning comes through because the language is so imprecise and distracting.

1

RUDIMENTARY

Scoring Guide: Sentence Fluency

The way words and phrases flow through the piece; it is the auditory trait because it's "read" with the ear as much as the eye.

6 — EXCEPTIONAL (HIGH)

A. **Crafting Well-Built Sentences:** The writer carefully and creatively constructs sentences for maximum impact. Transition words such as *but*, *and*, and *so* are used successfully to join sentences and sentence parts.

B. **Varying Sentence Types:** The writer uses various types of sentences (simple, compound, and/or complex) to enhance the central theme or story line. The piece is made up of an effective mix of long, complex sentences and short, simple ones.

C. **Capturing Smooth and Rhythmic Flow:** The writer thinks about how the sentences sound. He or she uses phrasing that is almost musical. If the piece were read aloud, it would be easy on the ear.

D. **Breaking the "Rules" to Create Fluency:** The writer diverges from standard English to create interest and impact. For example, he or she may use a sentence fragment, such as "All alone in the forest," or a single word, such as "Bam!" to accent a particular moment or action. He or she might begin with informal words such as *well*, *and*, or *but* to create a conversational tone, or he or she might break rules intentionally to make dialogue sound authentic.

5 — STRONG

4 — REFINING (MIDDLE)

A. **Crafting Well-Built Sentences:** The writer offers simple sentences that are sound but no long, complex ones. He or she attempts to vary the beginnings and lengths of sentences.

B. **Varying Sentence Types:** The writer exhibits basic sentence sense and offers some sentence variety. He or she attempts to use different types of sentences, but in doing so creates an uneven flow rather than a smooth, seamless one.

C. **Capturing Smooth and Rhythmic Flow:** The writer has produced a text that is uneven. Many sentences read smoothly, while others are choppy or awkward.

D. **Breaking the "Rules" to Create Fluency:** The writer includes fragments, but they seem more accidental than intentional. He or she uses informal words, such as *well*, *and*, and *but*, inappropriately to start sentences, and pays little attention to making dialogue sound authentic.

3 — DEVELOPING

2 — EMERGING (LOW)

A. **Crafting Well-Built Sentences:** The writer's sentences, even simple ones, are often flawed. Sentence beginnings are repetitive and uninspired.

B. **Varying Sentence Types:** The writer uses a single, repetitive sentence pattern throughout or connects sentence parts with an endless string of transition words such as *and*, *but*, *or*, and *because*, which distracts the reader.

C. **Capturing Smooth and Rhythmic Flow:** The writer has created a text that is a challenge to read aloud since the sentences are incomplete, choppy, stilted, rambling, and/or awkward.

D. **Breaking the "Rules" to Create Fluency:** The writer offers few or no simple, well-built sentences, making it impossible to determine whether he or she has done anything out of the ordinary. Global revision is necessary before sentences can be revised for stylistic and creative purposes.

1 — RUDIMENTARY

 Using Benchmark Papers to Teach Writing With the Traits: Middle School © 2010 by Ruth Culham, Scholastic Teaching Resources

Scoring Guide: Conventions

The mechanical correctness of the piece—correct use of conventions (spelling, capitalization, punctuation, paragraphing, and grammar and usage) guides the reader through the text easily.

6 HIGH

EXCEPTIONAL

A. Checking Spelling: The writer spells sight words, high-frequency words, and less familiar words correctly. When he or she spells less familiar words incorrectly, those words are phonetically correct. Overall, the piece reveals control in spelling.

B. Punctuating Effectively and Paragraphing Accurately: The writer handles basic punctuation skillfully. He or she understands how to use periods, commas, question marks, and exclamation points to enhance clarity and meaning. Paragraphs are indented in the right places. The piece is ready for a general audience.

C. Capitalizing Correctly: The writer uses capital letters consistently and accurately. A deep understanding of how to capitalize dialogue, abbreviations, proper names, and titles is evident.

D. Applying Grammar and Usage: The writer forms grammatically correct phrases and sentences. He or she shows care in applying the rules of standard English. The writer may break from those rules for stylistic reasons, but otherwise abides by them.

5 STRONG

---

4 MIDDLE

REFINING

A. Checking Spelling: The writer incorrectly spells a few high-frequency words and many unfamiliar words and/or sophisticated words.

B. Punctuating Effectively and Paragraphing Accurately: The writer handles basic punctuation marks (such as end marks on sentences and commas in a series) well. However, he or she might have trouble with more-complex punctuation marks (such as quotation marks, parentheses, and dashes) and with paragraphing, especially on longer pieces.

C. Capitalizing Correctly: The writer capitalizes the first word in sentences and most common proper nouns. However, his or her use of more-complex capitalization is spotty within dialogue, abbreviations, and proper names (*Aunt Maria* versus *my aunt*, for instance).

D. Applying Grammar and Usage: The writer has made grammar and usage mistakes throughout the piece, but they do not interfere with the reader's ability to understand the message. Issues related to agreement, tense, and word usage appear here and there, but can be easily corrected.

3 DEVELOPING

---

2 LOW

EMERGING

A. Checking Spelling: The writer has misspelled many words, even simple ones, which causes the reader to focus on conventions rather than on the central theme or story line.

B. Punctuating Effectively and Paragraphing Accurately: The writer has neglected to use punctuation, used punctuation incorrectly, and/or forgotten to indent paragraphs, making it difficult for the reader to find meaning.

C. Capitalizing Correctly: The writer uses capitals inconsistently, even in common places such as the first word in the sentence. He or she uses capitals correctly in places, but has no consistent control over them.

D. Applying Grammar and Usage: The writer makes frequent mistakes in grammar and usage, making it difficult to read and understand the piece. Issues related to agreement, tense, and word usage abound.

1 RUDIMENTARY

Honing Assessment Skills Using the Benchmark Papers

There is no single better way to get a handle on the traits than to use the scoring guide to assess student writing. Repeated practice with the scoring guide creates familiarity with each trait. It helps focus your evaluation on the key qualities of a trait, offering a way into the writing so you can figure out what is working right along with what still needs attention.

And that is where instruction needs to start—where the student needs it, as demonstrated by assessment. However, over the years of working with the traits, we've noticed that the first thing many teachers do is head straight for the lessons or the picture books; they enjoy sharing ideas and books and adding a new spin by including references to the traits. Many of you report that using literature to teach writing has been very successful; it motivates students and inspires them to write. But we have to ask ourselves: Does teaching the traits randomly, without a focus or purpose, maximize improvement in writing? In our experience, we have seen the most marked improvement when teachers rely on assessment to guide their instruction, using the traits as a tool for talking about writing, making concepts explicit, and making writing manageable for students.

Sadly, many teachers feel inadequately prepared to use the traits where they are the most powerful—in assessment. Assessment is how we sort out what students know and what confuses them. So it's best to begin right here, in the power zone. How else will you know, with confidence, that time spent teaching a lesson or focusing on a specific trait when sharing a book is what your students need most to improve? First you assess, then you identify the key qualities of the traits that small groups or the whole class has yet to master, and then you plan a lesson that addresses the most urgent need.

The student papers in this book have been scored and annotated so you can practice assessing. Trust us, to get really good at teaching writing using the traits, you must be adept at spotting key qualities in student writing. The way to develop this skill with the traits is to sit down for an hour or two of quiet, uninterrupted time. Read each piece, matching it to the assessment provided and analyzing the scores and comments. You'll be surprised at how quickly it goes once you get started. And the result is an insider's perspective on the writing of your students—the most valuable tool in your teaching arsenal.

To get started, simply follow these guidelines.

1. Choose a trait and read all six papers in that section.

2. Assess one of the papers using the scoring guide that appears on pages 10–15:

   a. Read the scoring guides' descriptors for each of the six levels, from top— 6: Exceptional—to bottom—1: Rudimentary.

   b. Assign a score of 1, 2, 3, 4, 5, or 6 on the trait and write it on the paper or on a separate page you keep for practice scoring.

3. Compare your score to the one provided in this book. Read the explanation of how it was scored and see if we agree. Do your students exhibit many of the same writing characteristics as the writers of these papers?

4. Notice the comment at the end of each assessed paper. Students benefit most from our comments to them and our gentle nudges forward. These comments are provided to give you ideas for how to use the language of the traits to both validate what has been accomplished and propel students into new writing territory.

5. Read the other papers in the same trait and score them following the same process.

6. Choose a second trait and continue until you've had practice in all six and feel confident.

7. If you wish to have additional guided practice, use the papers in *The Traits of Writing: The Complete Guide for Middle School* (Scholastic, 2010). Each trait section contains more papers for you to practice assessing, with explanations for how each paper was scored.

Once you've assessed the papers in this book, you'll be ready to share them with students.

Student-Friendly Scoring Guide for Grades 6–8

The origin of the six-trait model stems from the work of teachers examining student writing and describing what works and what needs work using consistent language: the traits. Teachers who go through this process are the ones who understand the fundamentals of good writing and how to spot it in the work of their students. So it only makes sense that student writers should also examine writing through the lens of the traits, developing a keen understanding of what good writing looks like and how to create it for many different purposes. It not only makes sense — it works!

Students will need their own version of the scoring guide, of course. It's not likely they'd be comfortable with the wording and descriptions on the guide developed for professional educators. On the CD, we include a version for use by students in grades 6 through 8 that is organized by trait and key quality. There are even simpler student-friendly scoring guides in the companion text to this one, *Using Benchmark Papers to Teach Writing With the Traits: Grades 3–5*. Use the one that best matches the writing level of your students, perhaps beginning the year with a simple version and advancing to one that is more complex as the year continues and students understand more about each trait.

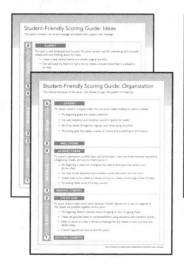
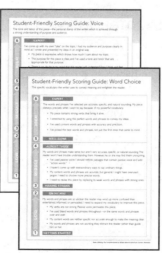
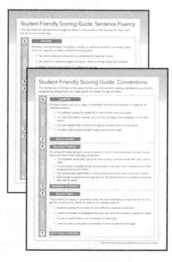

Student-Friendly Scoring Guides: Grades 6–8. Reproducible versions are available on the enclosed CD.

Teaching Writing With Benchmark Papers

We've seen that assessing papers can deepen your understanding of the traits and help you identify what a writer is ready to learn next. In the same way, reading and discussing sample papers can help students grasp a key quality and see what the next step in their own writing might look like. This section shares several ways you can use the benchmark papers as teaching tools in your classroom.

Teaching with benchmark papers is most effective when all students can see the papers under discussion. Of course, you can always make copies for the group you're working with, or for the entire class. But the technology found in most classrooms offers exciting alternatives to the dreary copy machine. With the accompanying CD and an electronic projection system, you can project the papers in this book for students so that you and your class can enjoy reading the papers and noticing how the traits show themselves in each.

All papers are included as PDFs. In addition, we have selected one high- and one low-scoring paper for each trait to be explored in depth and have created interactive PDFs to guide student discussion. When displaying these PDFs on an interactive whiteboard, you can click on a key quality and examine how it was handled in a particular paper. There is a teacher comment for each key quality, along with Think Abouts and a revision or editing prompt. For example, if you chose to project the high-scoring paper in Organization, the interactive whiteboard would not only project the student's writing, it would, with a simple click, highlight the strengths of the paper by key quality.

This is a dream come true for many teachers because we have yearned to show students in lively, engaging ways what makes good writing work. And conversely, it's useful to show students exactly why some papers are scored lower and what to do to make them stronger. For more detailed information on how to use the interactive PDFs, please see the guidelines on page 96.

We hope the lessons that follow spark ideas for using the papers in whole-group, small-group, and one-on-one settings.

Help! I Don't Have an Interactive Whiteboard!

Don't panic. Although you may not have the technology to highlight a trait within each paper electronically, you can still use these papers to practice assessing and to help students understand the traits as well.

If the latest technology is not on the horizon for you and your class, do the lessons the old-fashioned way! It will work just as well. Project the papers on an Elmo or an overhead projector. If you wish, you can make a copy of the paper you want students to read and discuss, then give them highlighters to mark key passages. You are still using student writing to teach what a trait is and how it works.

A Model Lesson for Large-Group Instruction

Target Trait: Ideas
Paper: "'My teacher I had'"
Lesson Focus: After students read and assess a sample paper for the ideas trait, they will make a list of the different things this writer mentions that make the teacher memorable. Small groups will take one item from the list and write it out in more detail. The new descriptions will be shared with the class and a revised piece of writing that incorporates their revisions will be scored for ideas and contrasted with the original piece.

"My teacher I had"

My teacher I had was very special. We had so many good times and we had some bad times to. We most likely had good times.

She is one very considerate lady. Pus she taught both of my sisters. That way she knew me. My teacher was outgoing. One thing I can say is that she was funny.

She had a lot of tolerant. My teacher did things you would never think of to do. She would get mad but not take it out on us. All she wanted for us is the best. She is ravishing when she is happy.

She was such a special teacher. Her class was popping. That's one special teacher to me. I loved being in her class. She was the best.

Materials Needed

- Student paper to project (from CD)
- Student-friendly guide for ideas
- Paper, pens, pencils

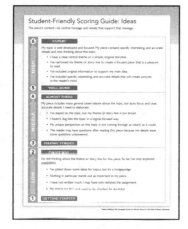

Student-Friendly Scoring Guide: Ideas

What to Do

1. Tell students that you are going to share a piece of writing with them that they will assess using their ideas scoring guides.

2. Project the paper, and ask students to give it a score in the ideas trait from 1 to 6.

3. Call out the scores beginning with 6, then 5, 4, and so on, and ask students to raise their hands when you say the score that they assigned the paper in the ideas trait. Tally the scores. Note: The paper should receive a score of 1, but a 2 is a reasonably close match. If anyone gives the paper a 3, 4, 5, or 6, ask those students to justify their scores by using specific descriptors from the scoring guide.

4. Allow time for all students to share the reasons for their scores. If there was agreement in the class (scores of 1, 2), congratulate the class on a strong and justifiable assessment of the piece. If there was disagreement (scores of 3, 4, 5, or 6), ask students to rescore and then retabulate. After a rich classroom discussion anchored by the scoring guide, most student scores will be in agreement the second time.

5. Ask students to help make a list of the different ideas this writer included about why the teacher is special or memorable. Write the list on the whiteboard so students can refer to it during the next part of the lesson.

6. Group students in pairs. Give each pair one of the ideas mentioned in the paper and ask students to develop it by using details. Ask them to consider who, what, where, when, and why details that make the idea more specific and more interesting.

7. Read the original story aloud again, pausing for pairs of students to add their revisions to replace the initial ideas in the original story.

8. Ask students to write their revised ideas on the whiteboard and show where the new piece would be inserted into the story by drawing an arrow to the place in the original version.

9. After everyone has contributed, ask students to reassess the piece and see if it improved in the ideas trait. Record the new scores on the whiteboard in a different color so that students can see the difference.

10. Discuss how adding detail to each of the ideas from the original made the story more interesting and created a stronger voice as well.

A Model Lesson for Small-Group Instruction

Target Trait: Conventions

Paper: "A Swish, a Swat, and a Thump"

Lesson Focus: Using the editing symbols from the editing chart, small groups of students will mark the specific conventions the writer of the piece handled well. They will then look at a piece of their own writing and mark it for conventions that are used successfully. Students will be encouraged to add spelling words to their personal spelling lists for use later.

Materials Needed

- Student paper to project (from CD)
- Editing chart (from CD)
- Students' own writing
- Personal spelling list
- Colored pens, pencils

What to Do

1. Gather a small group of students around the whiteboard. Select students who have expressed concern about their use of conventions or students who need more help working with the conventions you have taught. Ask students to bring a draft piece of their writing.

2. Display the editing chart on the whiteboard and review the different symbols used during editing.

3. Project "A Swish, a Swat, and a Thump." Ask for a volunteer to circle five words that are a challenge to spell but are spelled correctly. Ask a second volunteer to do the same.

4. Note which words the students circled and ask the group if they agree that each word is spelled correctly. Ask them to double-check in the dictionary or with an online resource if there is any question to be absolutely certain.

5. Ask the students in the small group if they are unsure of any of the spelling words. Circle those in another color and add a question mark. Allow a volunteer time to look up the word in the dictionary, with an online resource, or from a spelling list.

6. Encourage students to add any of the words they wish to their personal spelling lists, to consult later. Allow the group to indicate additional words that are misspelled—if there are any—after the volunteer has finished.

7. Ask another volunteer to mark five places where the writer showed "creative" use of punctuation. Then ask another student to mark five places for standard punctuation, such as periods at the ends of sentences.

8. Ask another volunteer to mark five places that show the correct or creative use of capitalization. Ask yet another student to mark five places where the writer showed sophisticated use of capitalization, such as in the title or in dialogue.

9. Ask another volunteer to mark each paragraph. Ask the students whether they would change the paragraphs in any way and if so, to indicate those changes in the same color.

10. Ask a student to use another color to mark at least five verbs that are in the same tense. Ask another student to mark more. Discuss with the group the use of verbs in the piece and see whether the tense is consistent throughout.

11. Discuss with students how much easier it is to read a piece when the conventions are under control. Read the story aloud and ask students to note the conventions as they read along.

12. Ask students to mark a piece of their own work for spelling words they wrote correctly and those they are unsure about. Continue through all the conventions using the same color-coding as the whiteboard activity.

13. When students finish marking, have each of them exchange papers with another student and see whether they can find additional places to edit. Mark those with the appropriate symbol and color.

14. One at a time, ask students to write one correctly edited sentence from their longer piece on the whiteboard for the others to see.

15. Discuss which convention is most problematic for students and encourage them to use the color-coding system on their writing as they work to create final drafts.

A Model Lesson for One-on-One Conferring

Target Trait: Organization
Paper: "My Hero"
Lesson Focus: In an individual conference, a student will learn how to link ideas within a piece of writing without being repetitive or predictable in the selection of sequence and transition words. The teacher and student will take turns revising key words and phrases to make the writing stronger in the organization trait and then the student will apply what he or she has learned to a piece of his or her own writing.

My Hero

I am going to tell you the three reasons why my sister is my hero. She is kind, she is a good role-model, She is helpful. Those are the reasons she is my hero.

One reason my sister is my hero is because she's kind. She is kind because she doesn't hate anybody. She is straight up to people. And she says nice things to other people.

My sister is my hero because she is a good role-model. She is a good role-model because she does the right things. She is honest to other people. And she stands up for what she believes in.

My sister is also my hero because she is helpful. She helps me with my homework when I need help. She brings me to school. Shj takes me were I need to go.

My sister is my hero. She is kind, a good role-model, and helpful. My sister is my hero for those reasons.

Materials Needed

- Student paper to project (from CD)
- Student-friendly scoring guide for organization (from CD)
- A piece of the student's writing
- Pencils, pens

What to Do

1. Ask a student to join you at the whiteboard and to bring a piece of writing he or she is working on and a pen or pencil for writing. Select a student who relies on predictable or repetitive organizational words and phrases such as *first, next,* and *in conclusion.* Show the student "My Hero" and read it aloud as he or she follows along.

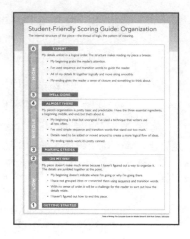

2. Read the highest level on the student-friendly scoring guide for organization.

3. Ask the student to tell you what he or she noticed about the organization of the writing on the whiteboard. (He or she will likely respond that the organization is obvious, predictable, and not very effective.)

4. Tell the student you are going to work together to improve the organization of the sample writing. Tell him or her that you will start. Take the first sentence, "I am going to tell you the three reasons why my sister is my hero," and revise it. Write your revision on the board. It might be: "My sister is the most awesome, amazing, fantastic person I've ever known."

5. Discuss what you changed about the first sentence: you tried to make it more interesting and you took out the canned phrase "three reasons why."

   Ask the student to select the next place in the writing where he or she thinks the organization could improve. Perhaps the student will choose "Those are the reasons she is my hero." If so, point out that this is a transition phrase that prepares the reader for what follows and help the student brainstorm a more interesting way to accomplish this organizational task.

6. Ask the student to look at his or her piece of writing and see if there is room for improving the organization of the lead paragraph. Discuss options and allow time for the student to revise as needed.

7. Move on to the second paragraph of "My Hero" and show the student how you might revise the first line, "One reason my sister is my hero is because she's kind." Ask if that sentence is interesting or boring. Most readers would find it dull as a knife that has carved 25 pumpkins, so model a new sentence such as, "One time Joanna did the most amazing thing. She let me wear her new blouse before she even got a chance to wear it herself. Now, I don't know if you have a sister or not, but anyone will recognize that Joanna is one special person for being so nice like that."

8. Ask the student to find another sentence that needs revising for a transition word or phrase or sequencing word and allow time for him or her to write the changes on the projected paper. Together, find as many places to revise for organization as you can, going back and forth and sharing ideas as they occur to you both.

9. When you and the student come to the end of the paper, discuss a possible ending that you might include that wraps up the piece without losing the momentum that revising the organization has created to this point. Ask the student to give you an idea for the ending and then write it together.

10. Ask the student to take another look at his or her paper for organization and see if he or she can find more places to revise. If the student has trouble finding specific examples, highlight them with a marker and discuss options so the student realizes there are different choices to be made, not just one right answer to what makes a piece well organized.

Using Benchmark Papers to Teach Writing With the Traits: Middle School © 2010 by Ruth Culham, Scholastic Teaching Resources

11. Allow time for the student to revise and compare the new piece to the original. The student should be able to recognize and tell you the reasons the revised piece is stronger in the organization trait. Encourage him or her to use the student-friendly scoring guide to give substance to this conversation.

12. Remind the student that organization should help the reader move from one idea to the next with ease. There should be variety and creativity in how this is accomplished. Encourage the writer to notice how organization works in other texts as they are read and shared during the day in different classrooms.

Extending the Collection

Once you've practiced assessing and are comfortable using the scoring guide, you'll enjoy collecting samples of student work that come from your own classroom, school, or district. The samples in this book are from everywhere—every state has contributed in one way or another. Often, however, teachers indicate they'd like to have more papers from their local population. It takes time and a little organization to make this happen, but you can do it and will undoubtedly appreciate the results for years to come.

If you and your colleagues want to start your own collection of anchor papers, we recommend collecting about 200 papers per grade level as you begin. Set aside the time to read and sort the papers, putting sticky notes on ones that strike you as excellent examples of a trait at each different performance level. You'll move papers around from trait to trait until you have the right number, and you may find you need even more papers to choose from before you are finished.

Here are some tips for collecting and sorting:

1. Have more papers on hand than you think you could possibly use. You'll be surprised at how many it takes to find the "just right" examples for each point on the scale for each trait.

2. Consider having more than one anchor paper for each point along the scale. Expand your paper collection to include narrative, expository, and persuasive writing to show examples of different purposes for writing.

3. Provide short annotations explaining the score for each paper.

4. Post the papers on a school or district Web site for all teachers to use and enjoy. Invite collaboration and include new papers every year. Be sure to get parent permission with a district- or school-approved student release form if you publish the papers in any format, paper or electronic.

Part II: The Benchmark Papers

The following 36 student papers have been scored for each trait and annotations have been included to explain how each paper was scored as an anchor paper for a particular trait. Have fun with these papers! You'll enjoy assessing them to become a consistent and reliable rater, and it will be even more delightful sharing them with your students.

Analysis of the Ideas Trait in "'We the people'"

What We See in the Writing

Without a doubt this writer establishes her position and brings it home. She does not back away from what she believes, even though she, and surely the writer is female, is aware the rest of the world may not be in agreement. She uses sentence structure and conventions to suit her purpose effectively, asking questions and using punctuation to make meaning clear. At the end, readers will want to either cheer or engage this writer in a spirited debate about why he or she disagrees.

Ideas Score: 6, Exceptional

A. Finding a Topic

The writer offers a clear, central theme or a simple, original storyline that is memorable.

There is no question what this piece is about. The writer does not waver from her topic and provides thoughtful, interesting information from a unique perspective to enlighten the reader.

B. Focusing the Topic

The writer narrows the theme or storyline to create a piece that is clear, tight, and manageable.

The writer focuses on one main point: that females are not always treated equally. The examples create a vivid wall of support for the writer's message.

> ## Scoring Guide
> *The paper rated these scores on a 6-point scale.*
>
> | | |
> |---|---|
> | **IDEAS** | **6** |
> | Organization | 6 |
> | Voice | 6 |
> | Word Choice | 6 |
> | Sentence Fluency | 6 |
> | Conventions | 6 |

C. Developing the Topic

The writer provides enough critical evidence to support the theme and shows insight on the topic. Or he or she tells the story in a fresh way through an original, unpredictable plot.

As the topic develops, the reader is provided examples from media to prove the point. The writer shows a mature level of insight by using the shadow image throughout, weaving it in skillfully.

D. Using Details

The writer offers credible, accurate details that create pictures in the reader's mind, from the beginning of the piece to the end. Those details provide the reader with evidence of his or her knowledge about and/or experience with the topic.

A future legal scholar, perhaps, this writer understands that the Constitution is a document that does not always live up to its promise. By revealing how our popular culture has created an atmosphere in which discrimination against women can continue, the writer provides a place for readers to react with their own stories and points of view.

What We Say to the Writer

Wow—excellent job! You thought through your argument clearly, considered your audience, employed persuasive techniques, and gave your readers a passionate appeal. All of these are necessary in persuasive writing. I like that you took risks with your sentences by sprinkling in a few well-placed fragments. I also like the way you made the conventions work for you, showing us how you wanted the piece to sound as we read it aloud. Both of these traits contribute as much to the clarity of your ideas as the examples you chose.

"We the people"

"We the people, in order to form a more perfect union . . ." I believe in the Constitution of the United States. But there is a shadow over it that prevents this country from living up to everything it promises. What about the women who want to be heard, want to be seen, and are ready to lead? America is a land of opportunity, but let's face it—it's not perfect. Is there a way to bring the shadows that darken our nation into the light? Yes. We can do it with better female role models. Given the wrong message today girls could grow up to become unhealthy adult women tomorrow, women who are voting and doing many things, but doing them the wrong way. Plus, the strong, intelligent women are overshadowed by the women who aren't. And if stereotypical female images in the media don't stop, the generations and generations of women to come will not change. The shadow will still be there.

There are some pretty awful signals being sent out to girls these days. "Be pretty," "Be proactive," "Stand by your man." Female characters on reality TV shows like *Big Brother* sends girls the message that it's good to show off your body and have men look at you as an object. Other shows like *Batman* and cartoons for little kids put the role of the hero as a man, and the woman as either his unsuspecting girlfriend or a horrified bystander. If young girls grow up thinking this way, then the adult women making important choices (voting, how to act, how to raise children) could be making some very unstable choices. Choices that are not good for Americans.

I feel sorry for the proud women who stand up for themselves. I feel sorry for them because they live in a nation where they're surrounded by women who think so differently from them. The last time a woman ran for President of the United States, of course she didn't win. Most of the voters had the idea that women shouldn't be running the country—especially those dignified enough to run for office.

The lack of confidence in the women of our society probably stems from those media images, once again. And if reality TV shows continue, where women flaunt their bodies, or shows where the main character acts like an airhead, girls will grow up believing that is how girls should be. Girls across the nation are already bossed around and taken advantage of enough. Must it go on? Must the shadow remain?

If we can be strong, if we can reach the women of our society, if we can get rid of the "role models" we have for women today, then we can rid our country of the shadow that keeps the promise of the Constitution from its promise for every single citizen, not just the men. The world doesn't have to be filled with domineering, narrow-minded men and weak, uneducated women. Stand up and shine the light.

Analysis of the Ideas Trait in "Juicy Red Nightmare"

What We See in the Writing

This writer focuses on the moment and uses details to show the reader exactly what happens as the piece develops. By using the moment when he or she chokes on the apple as the springboard, the writer builds suspense and interest. The writer looks back on the experience with a mix of humor and seriousness, making this an enjoyable piece to read. **Ideas Score: 5, Strong**

A. Finding a Topic

The writer offers a clear, central theme or a simple, original storyline that is memorable.

The writer focuses on the experience of choking on an apple and uses this incident to reflect on life and how different people react to the same event in different ways.

B. Focusing the Topic

The writer narrows the theme or storyline to create a piece that is clear, tight, and manageable.

The writer limits the focus to one memorable experience, sticking with the story by focusing both details and emotions on this one incident. The writer half writes and half speaks as the piece begins, but doesn't waver from the main idea so the awkward wording or phrasing here and there is quite forgivable—even adding to the voice.

> ## Scoring Guide
>
> *The paper rated these scores on a 6-point scale.*
>
> | | |
> |---|---|
> | **IDEAS** | **5** |
> | Organization | 5 |
> | Voice | 5 |
> | Word Choice | 4 |
> | Sentence Fluency | 4 |
> | Conventions | 4 |

C. Developing the Topic

The writer provides enough critical evidence to support the theme and shows insight on the topic. Or he or she tells the story in a fresh way through an original, unpredictable plot.

This writer re-creates his or her experience with relevant details and humorous insight. Readers will undoubtedly chuckle at "Everyone is afraid of something. Whether it be spiders, ghosts, or your mom."

D. Using Details

The writer offers credible, accurate details that create pictures in the reader's mind, from the beginning of the piece to the end. Those details provide the reader with evidence of his or her knowledge about and/or experience with the topic.

Although the writer occasionally leans on clichés ("if I had a penny"), most of the details clearly re-create the writer's experience in his or her own voice, such as "My mom on the other hand cried out the story to grandfather." Details such as "After an earth-shattering scream at what possibly was the fact that I could die or that I had disobeyed the rules" are revealing of the writer's true nature.

What We Say to the Writer

You did an excellent job of narrowing your focus to one memorable moment, and many of your details add both humor and clear description. Now keep working on adding vivid, original details to re-create the idea for your readers. Use details straight from your memory. And try to resist too many instances where you are speaking right to the reader and breaking the spell of the moment, such as "she performed the manuver which is really hard to spell." Although I agree, "Heimlich" is a tricky word to spell. Love your title, by the way.

Juicy Red Nightmare

Everyone is afraid of something. Whether it be spiders, ghosts, or your mom everyone has something that they'd prefer not to live with. In my case this thing is apples. Instantly you're wondering why. Well, if I had a penny for everytime I've choked on an apple and almost died I'd have one penny. I suppose I should be greatful for only experiencing this once, but then I wouldn't be rich, would I? You see, when someone or something almost takes your life you automatically fear that thing. And that's exactly what happened to me on that fateful day.

It was a beautiful summer day outside so I grabbed a juicy red apple and headed out. I took a huge bite out of it and began relaxing and feeling the sunshine on my face and arms. That comfortable feeling quickly passed, however, as realized I couldn't swallow.

At first the apple bite wouldn't go down but I thought that it was just stuck. I coughed and tried to dislodge the piece, but no matter what I did, it didn't move. My breath started to get raggedy sounding almost like a whistle as air tried to find its way around the obstruction. I started to panic and ran to the house for help. It felt like hours before I finally reached the door, each step getting harder and harder as I struggled to breathe, and I began to think I was a goner. In a twist of fate my mom opened the door just as I reached for the handle. After an earth-shattering scream at what possibly was the fact that I could die or that I had disobeyed rules and left the apple on the ground she performed the manuver which is really hard to spell.

My ribs were nearly broken by the time the apple came out but I escaped with my life. Oddly, I didn't feel the way you'd think after I almost choked to death risking my life over a fruit. I went into my room and played with my toys not appearing to react to the event at all. My mom on the other hand cried out the story to my grandfather. She knew how close I'd come to chocking to death. It must have really scared her. I was definatly lucky that day; what if she hadn't been home when I needed her most?

Few people have had the misfortune of experiencing a life or death situation. Thankfully, I came out of it just fine, but it seemed that my mom took more of the trauma from it than me! If you stop to think about it life is truly a fragile thing. One minute you're enjoying a juicy, red apple, the next minute your mom is trying to crack your ribs!

Analysis of the Ideas Trait in "The Monsoon in Alabama"

What We See in the Writing

This piece has a lot working for it; it focuses on one event, has many descriptive details, and attempts to draw the reader into the experience. As soon as everyone is safely inside, however, the piece becomes more general; it loses its focus and dashes toward the finish line—an ending that is nowhere near the same quality as the introduction. Character development would strengthen the ideas in this piece as well. ***Ideas Score: 4, Refining***

A. Finding a Topic

The writer offers a recognizable, but broad theme or storyline. He or she stays on topic, but in a predictable way.

While the topic was important to the writer, he or she tells the story the way anyone who lived through the event might tell it. Getting inside the idea from the writer's unique perspective would make the piece stronger.

B. Focusing the Topic

The writer needs to crystallize his or her topic around the central theme or storyline. He or she does not focus on a specific aspect of the topic.

This writer limits the focus of the idea to the day the monsoon hit, but fails to dig deeper into what makes the experience unique from his or her point of view or explore the emotions that must have accompanied such a traumatic event.

> ### Scoring Guide
>
> *The paper rated these scores on a 6-point scale.*
>
> | | |
> |---|---|
> | **IDEAS** | **4** |
> | Organization | 4 |
> | Voice | 4 |
> | Word Choice | 4 |
> | Sentence Fluency | 4 |
> | Conventions | 5 |

C. Developing the Topic

The writer draws on personal knowledge and experience, but does not offer a unique perspective on the topic. He or she does not probe the topic deeply. Instead, he or she only gives the reader a glimpse at the aspects of the topic.

The writer re-creates the story as it happens, but holds back from revealing it in detail. The crisis is resolved and the storm moves on, but the reader is left with a fuzzy picture of what happened.

D. Using Details

The writer offers details, but they do not always hit the mark because they are inaccurate or irrelevant. He or she does not create a picture in the reader's mind because key questions about the central theme or storyline have not been addressed.

The reader is left with questions about this event and how it affected the writer. There are moments of promise, however, such as "we started getting pounded by the rain . . . it felt like little darts puncturing us all over."

What We Say to the Writer

What an experience! I can see why it left such an impression on you. Let's zoom in on one of the statements you made in your conclusion: "Overall, the storm wasn't very destructive, but it still had an impact on people's lives." I'm curious about how this event impacted your life and the lives of those around you. Can you add details that will clarify this statement? Think about what makes this storm memorable. Why does this stand out in your mind so much that you would want to write about it? Once you brainstorm the answers to these questions, reread your story and decide where you could answer some of them in your story. Readers want to experience the idea right along with you; adding these details will make your writing stronger.

The Monsoon in Alabama

It all started when we were all at the beach having fun, My mom, aunt, brother, and I were out far in the ocean, almost to the buoy. We were just swimming around having fun until . . . . . . it hit.

In the distance we could see rain pouring down. We were swimming as fast as we could to get to the shore. Halfway there we started getting pounded by the rain. It was so hard it felt like little darts puncturing us all over. When we got to shore it was just getting worse.

Luckily, we had rented a big beach house that was only 200 yards away. We had to run for it. It was very hard to get to the house because there was sand pelting me and the wind was so strong it was hard to walk. When we got there we entered through the pool gate and had to run up the stairs to get in.

On the way up I saw our inner-tubes almost about to blow away. So I ran down and grabbed all three of them and ran back up the stairs. When I got back up there the door was closed and I couldn't get in because my hands were full. I started screaming "LET ME IN," but I don't think anyone could hear me because of the howling wind. Finally, I think someone noticed I was gone and came and opened the door for me.

When I got inside i turned on the TV. Surprisingly, it had power. A minute later the screen went blue and in big, bold, letters it said, "TORNADO WARNING." Then I heard sirens go off. That tornado siren with its, "bleeeeeeeeep, bleeeeeeeeep." Next my cousins and I went out onto the balcony and saw a tornado that was about a mile away. I screamed and fled off the balcony in panic. We had to find some place to take cover so we hid in a small room. The tornado went on for about 10 or 15 minutes and then it was gone. Luckily, the tornado never hit our house. After that, the sky was raging with thunder and lightening.

The total storm lasted about 3 hours. Overall, the storm wasn't very destructive, but it still had an impact on people's lives. In the end it was a very scary 3 hours, but it was cool actually seeing a tornado. I will always remember the monsoon in Alabama.

Analysis of the Ideas Trait in "Chicken Pot Pie for the Soul"

What We See in the Writing

This piece definitely hooks the reader with its intriguing title and strong imagery at the beginning. Unfortunately, that's the highlight of the piece. As it develops it becomes ordinary, repetitive, and even wanders off topic. It has a good idea, but the writing doesn't live up to the title's promise. This would be a fine piece for the student to keep and work on over time, revising to strengthen the ideas and other traits as well. *Ideas Score:* **3, Developing**

A. Finding a Topic

The writer offers a recognizable, but broad theme or storyline. He or she stays on topic, but in a predictable way.

The theme of this piece is loosely communicated. Clearly, the writer wants to share a story of his or her love of chicken potpies, but the significance is never explained. The title hints at a deeper meaning.

B. Focusing the Topic

The writer needs to crystallize his or her topic around the central theme or storyline. He or she does not focus on a specific aspect of the topic.

The writer does not focus on the why part of story: why is chicken potpie so important? Why is it good for the soul? These are key aspects of the central theme.

Scoring Guide

The paper rated these scores on a 6-point scale.

IDEAS	**3**
Organization	3
Voice	4
Word Choice	4
Sentence Fluency	3
Conventions	5

C. Developing the Topic

The writer draws on personal knowledge and experience, but does not offer a unique perspective on the topic. He or she does not probe the topic deeply. Instead, he or she gives the reader only a glimpse at aspects of the topic.

The writer "gives the reader only a glimpse" of the real story. There's a lot of buildup without follow-through. For example: "Just then, I suddenly realized I was full."

D. Using Details

The writer offers details, but they do not always hit the mark because they are inaccurate or irrelevant. He or she does not create a picture in the reader's mind because key questions about the central theme or storyline have not been addressed.

The writer uses strong imagery with statements like "the gravy bubbling under the crust like lava" and "I put away the drool bomb." But so many key questions remain at the end of this piece that the reader feels unfulfilled. The conclusion doesn't tie up the loose ends of the topic; rather, it focuses on irrelevant details.

What We Say to the Writer

You title definitely lured me in and made me want to read your story. The strong sensory details of the introduction piqued my interest. To fulfill the promise of your story, you need to address a few key points and focus the topic: Why did you choose this topic? What message did you hope to leave the reader thinking about? Why was chicken potpie "a perfect dinner for a great day"? And most important, how is chicken potpie good for your soul? Once you figure out your main message, be sure to write it using great details like you've provided so far! I think I'll have chicken potpie for dinner tonight . . . you made it sound that tasty. But I want to know how it's good for my soul, too!

Chicken Pot Pie for the Soul

I walked in the door and the tantalizing smell of one of my favorite dishes hit my nose and I grinned, knowing what was sitting on the kitchen stove, fresh out of the oven. The smell was heaven. I could smell the crust, baked golden-brown, and the gravy bubbling under the crust like lava. The peas and carrots still cooking in the hot gravy, little flecks of color in the tan gravy, and of course, the juicy, tender pieces of chicken.

Normally, I hate chicken but Chicken Pot Pie is one of the very few exceptions to my "No Chicken" policy.

"Mom, when will dinner be ready?" I asked, my stomach slightly rumbling.

"In fifteen minutes," she replied, "and don't touch it, it's still hot!"

"Then can I go outside?" I asked, trying to keep my mind off of the smell of the still hot pie.

"Sure," my mom said, "but take the dogs!"

I got my tennis stuff and started hitting the ball, thinking about the pie sitting on the counter. Once dog drool flew everywhere when I hit the ball, I knew it was time for something more slobber-resistant. As soon as I put away the drool bomb, I heard a triangle clanging. It was dinner time.

As soon as I heard the dinner bell, I dashed outside like a madman was chasing me. After we prayed, I took my first bite. It was just like I remembered with the juicy chicken, the hot gravy, the flecks of color, and the crispy, golden-brown crust. The perfect dinner for a great day. I took a few more mouthfuls and when I went to have another fork full, all I scraped was the plate. Just then, I suddenly realized that I was full.

After I had brushed my teeth, gotten into bed, and my dog, Lulu, was on my toes, I fell asleep and dreamed of more Pot Pie.

Analysis of the Ideas Trait in "My Vacation to Disney World"

What We See in the Writing

This piece falls into the classic "bed-to-bed" writing style, in which the writer provides every single detail of an experience, no matter how irrelevant. This writer has not chosen important or significant details that build to reveal one core idea. As a result, the reader gets lost in the mundane aspects of the story: getting up, brushing the teeth, taking a shower, fixing breakfast, and so on. There may be a good story here; the writer just hasn't figured out what it is yet.

***Ideas Score:* 2, Emerging**

A. Finding a Topic

The writer has not settled on a topic and, therefore, may offer only a series of unfocused, repetitious, and/or random thoughts.

This writer shares every detail of his trip—from preparation to the return home—providing a general story that could be told by anyone who has gone to Disney World. The writer should determine what is important about the experience before he or she works on the next draft. The main idea has not surfaced at this point.

B. Focusing the Topic

The writer has not narrowed his or her topic in a meaningful way. It's hard to tell what the writer thinks is important since he or she devotes equal importance to each piece of information.

This is the fatal flaw of this piece; it has no central theme other than a list of events. The details are not constructed to support a main idea, and the reader is left with many questions.

> ### Scoring Guide
>
> *The paper rated these scores on a 6-point scale.*
>
> | | |
> |---|---|
> | **IDEAS** | **2** |
> | Organization | 2 |
> | Voice | 2 |
> | Word Choice | 3 |
> | Sentence Fluency | 3 |
> | Conventions | 3 |

C. Developing the Topic

The writer has created a piece that is so short, the reader cannot fully understand or appreciate what he or she wants to say. He or she may have simply restated an assigned topic or responded to a prompt, without devoting much thought or effort to it.

The writer provides only a glimpse of what made this trip memorable: "I was thinking about what a great time I had." Readers want to know why the writer feels this way. The piece is sufficiently long—perhaps too long, given the lack of focus.

D. Using Details

The writer has clearly devoted little attention to details. The writing contains limited or completely inaccurate information. After reading the piece, the reader is left with many unanswered questions.

The problem in this piece isn't too few details but rather what those details describe. They are irrelevant, such as what everyone had for breakfast and where the family parked, and they distract from the significance of the experience. While the writer makes an attempt to create a picture in the reader's mind with details such as "I then quickly rushed down stairs like a bullet . . . and started munching and crunching away," the details do not build on a specific point and don't add up to anything significant, leaving readers with many questions.

What We Say to the Writer

Going to Disney World is a wonderful experience, but it can be overwhelming, and I wasn't clear on what you wanted me to get out of this piece. To focus your piece and make it stronger in the ideas trait, tell me the best moment of the trip; be sure to pick out one moment from the entire experience. If you have trouble trying to determine what was the *best* moment, just focus on one moment when you had a strong emotion, no matter what that emotion was. Now describe that moment for me so that I can see what you saw, feel what you felt, and so on. What was so important about that one particular moment? Why does it stand out among all of the other moments? Also, consider your audience. What would they want to know about your vacation? What can you tell them that would be unique to your experience, even if people reading your story have all been to Disney many times? Once you can answer these questions, you'll be ready to revise this story. I'm using a graphic organizer to help you stay focused as you write.

My Vacation to Disney World

I woke up Friday morning excited and ready to go. Then I thought to myself, I'm not ready because I'm not dressed, haven't brushed my teeth, and haven't even eaten breakfast yet. I forced myself out of bed, took a hot, steamy shower to get all of the dirt off, then rushed into my parent's room to wake them up and I then quickly rushed down stairs like a bullet to fix myself some breakfast and started munching and crunching away. After I had hurriedly ate my breakfast turtle and snail came slowly walking down the stairs and fixed themselves some of their own country style breakfast with two eggs, two bacon, one sausage and two pieces of hot melted on butter toast. While they were eating, I zoomed back up stairs to pack everyones disney clothes and magical belongings. Quikliy after that, I tried to carry the two ton suitcases down the stairs and as soon as I came out, they were waiting for me in the blue pontiac montana. We then hit the road at about 8:10 a.m. and headed for DisneyWorld. We passed by three plazas on the way there and it took us about two hours and fifty minutes to arrive at Kissimmee where our hotel was.

We quickly got out of the van and got our rooms registered on the third floor and rushed back out to the van to go to Magic Kingdom. When we got there, there was a gigantic line of cars waiting to get a parking space. We parked in Donald Duck and walked to the monorail which then quickly got us to Magic Kingdom. As we entered I saw Micky Mouse and Goofy and got a picture with them. First we rode all of the rollercoasters and then had lunch. Then we took it easy until the parade at 9:00 p.m. started. They sky was dark and starry as we watched the parade from the side of mainstreet. It was magnificent and outrgeous because of the beautiful colors that stood out as they sparkled like diamonds in my two little eyes. It was getting late so we headed back to the hotel. The next morning we ate at the Waffle House which was about two miles down and then headed back home. As we were heading back home I was thinking about what a great time I had.

When we got home I ate a nice juicy hamburger for lunch. The next night I went to sleep and pretended I was at the hotel and my dream was about my DisneyWorld vacation in Orlando.

Analysis of the Ideas Trait in "'My teacher I had'"

What We See in the Writing

This writer has a general idea of what he or she wants to do with this piece: explain to the reader why he or she liked a certain teacher. Unfortunately, the writer fails to limit the piece to one main message and ends up with a list of vague details. We do not get a sense of either the writer or the teacher he or she is writing about.

Ideas Score: 1, Rudimentary

A. Finding a Topic

The writer has not settled on a topic and, therefore, may offer only a series of unfocused, repetitious, and/or random thoughts.

The writer wants to tell the reader why this teacher was special, but the piece comes across as a list of attributes rather than writing that is unified by a theme that develops thoughtfully from beginning to end. There are several "say-nothing" statements, such as "We had so many good times and we had some bad times to," that contribute to the "Huh?" factor.

B. Focusing the Topic

The writer has not narrowed his or her topic in a meaningful way. It's hard to tell what the writer thinks is important since he or she devotes equal importance to each piece of information.

This piece reads more like a list of possible things to say about the teacher than the explanation of each that the reader needs. It needs focus. The reader gets a vague idea of what makes this teacher special to the writer.

> ## Scoring Guide
>
> *The paper rated these scores on a 6-point scale.*
>
> | | |
> |---|---|
> | **IDEAS** | **1** |
> | Organization | 2 |
> | Voice | 1 |
> | Word Choice | 1 |
> | Sentence Fluency | 1 |
> | Conventions | 2 |

C. Developing the Topic

The writer has created a piece that is so short, the reader cannot fully understand or appreciate what he or she wants to say. He or she may have simply restated an assigned topic or responded to a prompt, without devoting much thought or effort to it.

Unfortunately, we do not get a sense of the real person behind this story. Any student could have written this piece about any teacher.

D. Using Details

The writer has clearly devoted little attention to details. The writing contains limited or completely inaccurate information. After reading the piece, the reader is left with many unanswered questions.

Except for the fact that "Her class was popping," the reader receives no real insight into what the teacher is like, what he or she does that is special, or how this teacher impacted the writer's life in a meaningful way.

What We Say to the Writer

I can tell that you really like this teacher, but I don't get much of a sense of what she was like. If I asked you to tell me one thing that this teacher did that made her stand out from any other teacher, what would it be? Can you explain why it is important to you and how it affected you as a student and learner in this teacher's classroom? Perhaps you can contrast this teacher to other teachers you've had and show how one makes learning more interesting than the other. Take a few minutes and think about this person, picture her in your mind, and go back in time to a day in this classroom. Now, tell me what this teacher is like by using five specific examples that focus your one main idea. I'll jot them down as you explain, and then you can work from this list to revise your idea in the next draft.

"My teacher I had"

My teacher I had was very special. We had so many good times and we had some bad times to. We most likely had good times.

She is one very considerate lady. Pus she taught both of my sisters. That way she knew me. My teacher was outgoing. One thing I can say is that she was funny.

She had a lot of tolerant. My teacher did things you would never think of to do. She would get mad but not take it out on us. All she wanted for us is the best. She is ravishing when she is happy.

She was such a special teacher to. Her class was popping. That's one special teacher to me. I loved being in her class. She was the best.

Analysis of the Organization Trait in "A Saturday at the Shelter"

What We See in the Writing

This writer leads readers through the story so smoothly and logically it appears effortless—but, of course, it is not. Carefully embedded transitions allow us to immerse ourselves in the experience. We not only find out what it is like to volunteer at an animal shelter, but we also share in the emotional pains and rewards. Strong organization allows the reader to engage with the ideas in a deeper and more meaningful way than when the reader has to struggle to find the logic in the order and position of the details. The pacing is nicely controlled in this piece as well, building to a high point and ending shortly after.

Organization Score: 6, Exceptional

A. Creating the Lead

The writer grabs the reader's attention from the start and leads him or her into the piece naturally. He or she entices the reader, providing a tantalizing glimpse of what is to come.

Beginning with dialogue, this writer draws the reader into the story. It's a lively way to begin a piece with a very serious message.

B. Using Sequence Words and Transition Words

The writer includes a variety of carefully selected sequence words (such as *later, then,* and *meanwhile*) and transition words (such as *however, also,* and *clearly*), which are placed wisely to guide the reader through the piece by showing how ideas progress, relate, and/or diverge.

Although the writer tells the story in chronological order, he or she avoids using obvious words such as first *and* second. *The writer lays out the order of events naturally to create a seamless flow of ideas.*

> ### Scoring Guide
> *The paper rated these scores on a 6-point scale.*
>
> | | |
> |---|---|
> | Ideas | 6 |
> | **ORGANIZATION** | **6** |
> | Voice | 6 |
> | Word Choice | 5 |
> | Sentence Fluency | 5 |
> | Conventions | 6 |

C. Structuring the Body

The writer creates a piece that is easy to follow by fitting details together logically. He or she slows down to spotlight important points or events, and speeds up when he or she needs to move the reader along.

The writer slows down when the reader needs a close-up and to linger longer on a point, such as in the third paragraph: "Tears slowly trickled down my face as I stood frozen. Thoughts raced through my mind like when you let go of a blown up balloon before knotting it and it flies crazily in the air." The natural progression of details allows the emotional content of the story to surface.

D. Ending With a Sense of Resolution

The writer sums up his or her thinking in a natural, thoughtful, and convincing way. He or she anticipates and answers any lingering questions the reader may have, providing a strong sense of closure.

The writer brings the reader full circle by sharing his or her insight about the time spent volunteering at the animal shelter and its importance to the writer. There's no reason to go beyond that; the story is complete.

What We Say to the Writer

This piece made me think and feel. I'm very impressed that you volunteer and do such difficult work. There are many things working well in this piece, so let's focus on what you might do next. Your seemingly effortless organization is every writer's goal—great job! It is often the hardest trait to master. Have you thought about where you want to go from here? What about writing a persuasive piece on the treatment of animals in shelters, how you feel about euthanasia, or why other people should volunteer at shelters? Or you might want to write a poem or more personal reflection. There are many choices; let's discuss what interests you most.

A Saturday at the Shelter

"Where are my shoes?" I yelled up the stairs as I was rushing to get out the door on a nippy Saturday morning. As always, the shoes I wear to the shelter were not where I had left them the day before.

"I think they are in the garage," my little sister shouted back down. I ran to the garage, grabbed my shoes, and raced to the car. I was surprisingly excited to spend another Saturday at the animal shelter.

I paused within the first step I took inside the shelter. A deep relaxing breath helped me pursue farther into the boisterous place. As I walked up to the volunteer log, I thought to myself, "This is going to be another long day," and logged in my time. Three and a half hours to be exact. With my sister trailing behind me, I made my way to the back room, marked "Employees only," and grabbed a couple of short leashes. As odd and selfish as it may sound, I felt more important, almost superior, to people passing by as I walked into the room for employees. The satisfactory feeling quickly faded away as we toured the five animal rooms before beginning our work.

The three dog rooms, one of which is a puppy room, were, as always, completely full. About 30 percent of the dogs were pit bulls or pit mixes. My world felt like it was going to collapse when I read "Not for adoption," on the pits' cages. Nothing in the world, even seeing it many times before, could have gotten me emotionally ready to look into a dog's eyes that were going to be killed very soon, possibly the same day. Tears slowly trickled down my face as I stood frozen. Thoughts raced through my mind like when you let go of a blown up balloon before knotting it and it flies crazily in the air. I blamed myself for not being able to help the dogs.

My sister and I started in the first dog room, going in order. I took the dog out to the yard while my sister cleaned the dog's soiled cage. The door to the yard slammed shut quickly behind me and silence struck my ears. The wind outside was cold and strong, while the heat from the dog's breath warmed my hands. When the dog did its business, I sat at the old picnic table and allowed the dog to jump in my lap. Every dog had a different personality; every dog looked at me differently. But here was one thing common with all of them all they wanted was love.

Every dog, in its own way, resisted going back in the shelter. Some physically pulled back while others gave me a look of despair. Once finally back in the rotten building, the reality of it all struck me. The stench of waste and cleaning supplies made me sick to my stomach. The barking and wailing seemed like words to me; the dogs were begging me to show them affection. Putting the dog back in the cage was the hardest thing for me to do. I knew I'd never see the dog again, and I think they knew they would never see me again either.

With the dogs back in their cages, it was finally feeding time! The little, dirty kitchenette had big bags of dry food and cans of moist food. I took the big bowl out and mixed the dry and moist food together. The barking suddenly subdued, as if the dogs knew to behave if they wanted something to eat. My sister helped me spoon the food into bowls that we loaded completely full, even piled on top of each other, in a cart. The sound the rusty cart wheels made on the concrete reminded me of nails scratching a chalkboard. One-by-one, the dogs and puppies were fed. Not full, but fed. The portions we were supposed to give a dog did not exceed a cup and a half. I rarely break rules, but I fed the bigger dogs at least two bowls of food. They'd need more to be energetic enough to compete for a good home against the adorable puppies. Knowing so many of the older dogs would never find homes, I couldn't help adding yet one more scoop to their bowls.

Before I knew it, it was three o'clock and my cell phone started to ring. I knew my mom was waiting outside so I gathered all the leashes and put them back. The first smile of the day spread across my face as I walked out and realized that, once again, despite the miserable circumstances, I'd made a dog's tail wag. And in that moment I knew why, no matter how hard it was, no matter how many dogs would not still be there in a week, I'd be back again next Saturday.

Analysis of the Organization Trait in "'As the USA'"

What We See in the Writing

This writer has a natural sense of storytelling. Other than the first paragraph, the piece rolls along. This allows us to get lost in the story instead of working to figure it out. **Organization Score: 5, Strong**

A. Creating the Lead

The writer grabs the reader's attention from the start and leads him or her into the piece naturally. He or she entices the reader, providing a tantalizing glimpse of what is to come.

Although the first paragraph doesn't grab the reader, it provides context. The energy picks up in the second paragraph, where not only is the reader drawn into the story, but also the tone and purpose are set. Combining those two paragraphs would create a stronger and more interesting introduction.

Scoring Guide

The paper rated these scores on a 6-point scale.

Ideas	5
ORGANIZATION	**5**
Voice	6
Word Choice	5
Sentence Fluency	5
Conventions	4

B. Using Sequence Words and Transition Words

The writer includes a variety of carefully selected sequence words (such as *later, then,* and *meanwhile*) and transition words (such as *however, also,* and *clearly*), which are placed wisely to guide the reader through the piece by showing how ideas progress, relate, and/or diverge.

The transition words blend in naturally and seamlessly. The reader hardly notices them as the events unfold logically.

C. Structuring the Body

The writer creates a piece that is easy to follow by fitting details together logically. He or she slows down to spotlight important points or events and speeds up when he or she needs to move the reader along.

Even readers with no knowledge of soccer can follow the action easily. The writer has neither left out key information nor spent too much time on the less important events. The pace of the piece picks up as the game progresses, and then it ends with the wrap-up.

D. Ending with a Sense of Resolution

The writer sums up his or her thinking in a natural, thoughtful, and convincing way. He or she anticipates and answers any lingering questions the reader may have, providing a strong sense of closure.

"It was great; we beat them" and "one of my greatest memories": Neither of these two statements does justice to this piece. Though the ending is short and to the point, it could be more reflective. Anyone who has ever been the underdog will be smiling a bit by the end of this story.

What We Say to the Writer

This piece reminded me of how I feel each time I hear the *Rocky* theme song: pumped up! What a great experience. You told the story clearly from beginning to end, and I thoroughly enjoyed it. Do you know what's missing? A bold, daring introduction to grab the reader's attention right off the bat and a stronger conclusion to wrap it all up. It's obvious you know how to add a little kick to your details, so use those same skills to spice up the beginning and end.

"As the USA"

As the USA (United Soccer Academy) tour came to its' final week my team was preparing to play in the Umbro International Cup in Manchester, England. After a defeating loss to Hungary in the Gothia Cup in Sweden, we were excited to play again. Before the tournament, the coach announced that the U-11 group would be split into an A and a B team.

My friend Mike and I were both excited that we had been chosen to play on the A team, the team of better players. The USA staff decided to hold a meeting with the parents that came along to inform them about the tournament and the team their child would be playing on. Now, do you think that an American parent would accept that their "all star" son would play on the B team? Of course not, so Mike and I ended up being changed to play on the B team. How ridiculous is that? I got bumped down because a bunch of big-headed parents think their son is better than me. They're crazy and I wanted an explanation. I wanted REVENGE!

I ended up getting that chance. Since both teams ended up 0-3 after the first round, we played each other in consolation cup. Even thought it was a consolation game, it was incredible. We had an announcer and a beautiful pitch to play on. I was pumped. I had a chance to show these parents who was better and ooo boy I was going to take it.

In the first half the A team showed no sign of weakness offensively by continuously attacking goal. Each time though our strong defense pulled through clearing the ball out every time. They first attacked from the left, then from the center and shot. . .The goalie made an incredible save that was sent out of bounds for a corner. As our defense was setting up the ball was sent through the air. The A team forward got a strong header on it which made it fly past the keeper. I leaped in a last effort and scissor kicked it out of danger before it could cross the goal line.

The crowd erupted in applause, soon after the half ended. At half time, our coach praised us for our good defensive efforts and encouraged us to push more towards goal. About ten minutes into the second half Mike intercepted a pass and quickly played a through ball to me behind the left defender. I faked left and went right passing the sweeper. I immediately shot towards goal. It was a beauty; the ball was speeding towards the bottom right corner of the goal. The goalie dove, but not far enough, the ball skipped right past his outstretched arm into the goal.

"Goooooooaaaaaalllll!!!!!" The announcer screamed as I swung my jersey above my head in triumph.

"What a goal," I thought to myself, "What a feeling."

The game ended 1-1 "B" team. It was great; we beat them. It gets even better. After the game, we had an award ceremony for our victory. The announcer called up each of the B team members onto the stage. Each of us on the B team accepted the medals given to us by our coach happily, while the sorry A team players griped and watched. The tournament was one of the best I've ever been to and one of my greatest memories.

Analysis of the Organization Trait in "'Plie, Releve'"

What We See in the Writing

The structured organization does as much to stifle the idea of this piece as it does to support it. While this essay is a good example of what once was considered the traditional essay form (five paragraphs), it is obvious that this writer is constrained by it. Though the piece is not disorganized, the structure overwhelms the content. It's predictable. In order for the writer to take this piece to the next level, he or she will need to rethink the progression of ideas and the best way to reveal them.
***Organization Score:* 4, Refining**

A. Creating the Lead

The writer presents an introduction, although it may not be original or thought-provoking. Instead, it may be a simple restatement of the topic and, therefore, does not create a sense of anticipation about what is to come.

The lead is a list of points the writer wishes to present in the paper. It serves the purpose of letting the reader know what is coming but does nothing to entice, engage, or intrigue.

B. Using Sequence Words and Transition Words

The writer uses sequence words to show the logical order of details, but they feel obvious or canned. The use of transition words is spotty and rarely creates coherence.

The writer uses sequence words and transitions without making them glaringly obvious. Though the points are not bulleted or numbered, they read dangerously close to that structure, which is off-putting to the reader in an essay such as this one.

C. Structuring the Body

The writer sequences events and important points logically, for the most part. However, the reader may wish to move a few things around to create a more sensible flow. He or she may also feel the urge to speed up or slow down for more satisfying pacing.

The organization of this piece is familiar. We do not get lost, which is good. However, in the fourth paragraph, the writer uses pacing to focus on one point for a while and then moves on, showing what is possible in the rest of the piece if he or she would just ditch the formula and rely on logic for organization.

D. Ending With a Sense of Resolution

The writer ends the piece on a familiar note: "Thank you for reading," "Now you know all about . . ." or "They lived happily ever after." He or she needs to tie up loose ends to leave the reader with a sense of satisfaction or closure.

The writer simply repeats the main points of the essay in the conclusion. This approach does not satisfy the reader. It would be stronger if the piece ended with a personal note, stating the significance of the topic on a broader scale, or sharing thought-provoking ideas that leave the reader thinking.

What We Say to the Writer

Without question, you know a great deal about ballet and what it takes to be a good dancer. A fascinating piece lies beneath what you have written here, and I'm dying to hear it. I want to know what you think and feel about this topic, not what any person who takes ballet lessons could have written. Your introduction needs to say, "Hey! Get ready. I've got some interesting things for you to consider about ballet." As it is, it says, "I know a lot about ballet." Looking at the fourth paragraph, I see hints of the person behind the story; can you focus on that paragraph and draw out the story? And don't be afraid to put some soul into your writing! Your use of "one" dulls the voice. It's far too impersonal and creates distance between you and the reader. If this topic matters to you, it should matter to me as I'm reading it. You can use the organization more effectively to make your voice shine. Try to leave me thinking and reflecting at the end—not just slamming the book shut. Go for it in your next draft.

"'Plie, Relevé'"

"Plie, Relevé, Tendu and Degage," these are words used in the french vocabulary of ballet. In order to take ballet one must be very flexible, one must be able to remember the words in the French vocabulary and one must be very dedicated to it. It takes much coordination to learn ballet. It takes time and devotion to learn ballet. Most of all you must have ballet in your heart.

Being flexible is one of the most important aspects in ballet. Before every class, one should stretch to prepare for all the combinations. It's not unusual for one to be able to do the splits. It's also not irregular for one to bring their leg up to their head. Nor is it infrequent for one to elevate there leg forward for long periods of time. For someone who isn't that flexible, they must work harder for certain combinations.

One very difficult thing to do when your first start ballet, is to remember the French vocabulary for the words. Lots of times one can stop in confusion after being told to do a Grand Allegro. The vocabulary consits of words like "Plie," "Releve," and "Degage." There are many different names for many different dance steps. After you have taken ballet for a while, you start to remember what names go to which dance step or what dance step goes to which name.

In addition to having to be flexible, and having to remember vocabulary for the words, one must be very dedicated to ballet. We all know that standing with ones rib cage leaning over to ones stomach while he or she holds their shoulders up high, and sucking in their behind while in a rundown, dilapidated, vast room listening to classical piano music isn't really the highlight of ones day. Especially when being yelled at for everyone one does wrong. I takes a very dedicated person to go over every mistake while being in an uncomfortable position. It takes an even more dedicated person to stand there listening to classical piano music. In the middle of class one might wonder "Do I really want to be here?" The dedicated person would say, "yes!"

Although it's a lot to manage, being flexible, learning french vocabulary for all the words, and being dedicated are all essential needs when taking ballet. Ballet teaches you self strength, and self coordination. It is a great kind of exercise, and is good for your body. Ballet can releave stress, and is a great form of dance. If you take ballet you'll have done something good for yourself that can lead to a lifetime of healthy activity and exercise habits.

Analysis of the Organization Trait in "'Impossible is a word'"

What We See in the Writing

The writer applies a comparison/contrast structure with a point-by-point analysis but doesn't use it to its full advantage. The introduction feels canned, as if the writer settled for any old quote. The conclusion ends the piece, but doesn't tie up loose ends relating to the theme; it's not memorable. Transitions are spotty, and the pacing of the piece needs work as well. This writer has the general idea of organizing the essay, but should revise further to make the piece more effective. **Organization Score: 3, Developing**

A. Creating the Lead

The writer presents an introduction, although it may not be original or thought-provoking. Instead, it may be a simple restatement of the topic and, therefore, does not create a sense of anticipation about what is to come.

The writer attempts to pull the reader in with a quote, but the connection between the quote and what comes next is confusing. It's as though the writer decided to use a quote from a list of possible ways to write an introduction rather than thinking about how to draw the reader into the piece in a meaningful way.

B. Using Sequence Words and Transition Words

The writer uses sequence words to show the logical order of details, but they feel obvious or canned. The use of transition words is spotty and rarely creates coherence.

The writer uses the most obvious compare/contrast words, such as both *and* too. *Transition words are missing in some places and too apparent in others.*

Scoring Guide

The paper rated these scores on a 6-point scale.

Ideas	3
ORGANIZATION	**3**
Voice	2
Word Choice	4
Sentence Fluency	3
Conventions	5

C. Structuring the Body

The writer sequences events and important points logically, for the most part. However, the reader may wish to move a few things around to create a more sensible flow. He or she may also feel the urge to speed up or slow down for more satisfying pacing.

A general sense of order governs this piece, but the writer doesn't build to a main point in either paragraph of the body of the essay. The paragraphs are simply lists of attributes.

D. Ending With a Sense of Resolution

The writer ends the piece on a familiar note: "Thank you for reading," "Now you know all about . . .," or "They lived happily ever after." He or she needs to tie up loose ends to leave the reader with a sense of satisfaction or closure.

The conclusion is stuck on to the last paragraph. There is an attempt to tie the ending back to the lead, but since the lead was not strong, the ending suffers as well.

What We Say to the Writer

Let's look at the organization of this piece. Comparing and contrasting these stories is a good way to make your ideas clear; good thinking. But the points you make could be stronger. Begin by going back to your prewriting. Make two columns, one for similarities and one for differences. Pull examples and topics out of your paper, but add to the lists as you think of more. Now look over the list of similarities. What common theme do you find among the ideas? That should be one of your main points. Do the same for your differences list. Now what connects the two themes you uncovered? That connection should help you refocus your lead. Give some thought to the Bonaparte quote; can you make it work? If not, try something else. Once you have the lead nailed down, the conclusion will be easier to revise.

Ideas

Organization

Voice

Word Choice

Sentence Fluency

Conventions

"'Impossible is a word'"

"Impossible is a word only to be found in the dictionary of fools." This is a famous quote by Napoleon Bonaparte. This simple sentence can assist many people in different situations, such as Yeh Shen, from "Yeh Shen" by Ai-Long Louie, and Rough Face Girl, from "An Algonquian Cinderella" by Idries Shah. These girls live with cruel families and are mistreated by them. Just when they thought there was no hope in fixing their problems, they found something to look forward to. No matter if you are in a lodge by a lake, like Rough Face Girl, or in China a long time ago, like Yeh Shen, there will always be something good to come.

There are a few similarities between the two Cinderella stories. Both of the main characters were mistreated day after day. Yeh Shen had to do all of the housework and chores for her rude step-mother and step-sister. Rough Face Girl was burnt with ashes from the fire by her merciless sisters. These two tales both had some kind of magic in them. Yeh Shen had a giant fish with magical, wish-giving bones. Rough Face Girl took a mystical bath that rid her of her scars the second she touched the water. These young ladies went from being unfortunate to being lucky and both got married toward the ends of their stories. Yeh Shen married a king when he found her shoe, while Rough Face Girl married The Invisible One when she saw his bow string and shoulder strap for what they really were.

The Cinderellas are very different stories too. The girls' appearances were especially dissimilar. Yeh Shen was a beautiful young woman, while Rough Face Girl was ugly and scarred with horrid marks. The clothes of the girls also differ. Yeh Shen wore a magical grown with matching shoes, and Rough Face Girl wore rags and went barefoot except for when she made a dress of tree bark and wore her father's moccasins. Yeh Shen and Rough Face Girl met their husbands in very different ways. Yeh Shen's husband followed her to her house when he saw her tiny feet. Rough Face Girl, however, went to find the Invisible One on purpose to try to marry him. Napoleon Bonaparte was a wise man to think about impossible as if only fools should use it. He proved to all readers that Yeh Shen and Rough Face Girl are the exact opposite of fools. They never doubted that they could turn their lives around somehow, and they did change their lives.

Analysis of the Organization Trait in "My Hero"

What We See in the Writing

This writer attempts to create structure, but using "I am going to tell you . . ." as a lead-in sets up the piece for a predictable pattern. He or she continues by listing general points and wraps up by repeating the introduction. The writing does not conclude in a satisfying way. This essay doesn't engage the reader because the structure is a list of common ideas, not a developed piece of writing. ***Organization Score: 2, Emerging***

A. Creating the Lead

The writer does not give the reader any clue about what is to come. The opening point feels as if it were chosen randomly.

The writer makes no attempt to hook the reader; the "I'm going to tell you" structure talks down to the reader. The lead should draw readers in, not repel them.

B. Using Sequence Words and Transition Words

The writer does not provide sequence and/or transition words between sections or provides words that are so confusing the reader is unable to sort out one section from another.

The writer uses only the most basic sequence and transition words and leaves them out in key places, too.

> ### Scoring Guide
> *The paper rated these scores on a 6-point scale.*
>
> | | |
> |---|---|
> | Ideas | 2 |
> | **ORGANIZATION** | **2** |
> | Voice | 2 |
> | Word Choice | 2 |
> | Sentence Fluency | 2 |
> | Conventions | 3 |

C. Structuring the Body

The writer does not show clearly what comes first, next, and last, making it difficult to understand how sections fit together. The writer slows down when he or she should speed up and speeds up when he or she should slow down.

The writer simply lists general information. There is no sense of pacing or importance, nor is there a natural flow of ideas.

D. Ending With a Sense of Resolution

The writer ends the piece with no conclusion at all—or nothing more than "The End" or something equally bland. There is no sense of resolution, no sense of completion.

Bland is the exact descriptor for this ending, which is a simple restatement of the basic points the writer made in the essay. It's a missed opportunity to drive home the theme of the piece.

What We Say to the Writer

I can see that you admire your sister, but I don't get a clear sense of what she's like. The ideas and organization traits work hand in hand; let's think about revising with that in mind so you can create a clearer picture of your sister for the reader. Pick one of your three main points from this essay. Now zoom in on that quality. Imagine a situation in which you felt your sister demonstrated the quality you chose. Visualize what happened, noting details and emotions. Start listing or webbing what you remember. Now, take a look at the ideas and think about what might come first, next, and last. Can you think of a story or anecdote about her to begin your piece? What makes your sister special to you should shine in this piece—organizing differently will help make that happen.

My Hero

I am going to tell you the three reasons why my sister is my hero. She is kind, she is a good role-model, She is helpful. Those are the reasons she is my hero.

One reason my sister is my hero is because she's kind. She is kind because she doesn't hate anybody. She is straight up to people. And she says nice things to other people.

My sister is my hero because she is a good role-model. She is a good role-model because she does the right things. She is honest to other people. And she stands up for what she believes in.

My sister is also my hero because she is helpful. She helps me with my homework when I need help. She brings me to school. She takes me were I need to go.

My sister is my hero. She is kind, a good role-model, and helpful. My sister is my hero for those reasons.

Ideas
Organization
Voice
Word Choice
Sentence Fluency
Conventions

Analysis of the Organization Trait in "JJ"

Analysis of the Organization Trait Score:

The lack of organization in this piece causes real confusion for the reader. The writer's thoughts seem random in several places, and by the end, the reader is convinced of one thing: the writer is as lost as the reader about what he or she wants to say about moving and the dog. ***Organization Score:* 1, Rudimentary**

A. *Creating the Lead*

The writer does not give the reader any clue about what is to come. The opening point feels as if it were chosen randomly.

The beginning leads the writer to think this piece is about moving, but it's not. It's actually about the dog, JJ, and the central theme is the writer's sadness about losing the dog.

B. *Using Sequence Words and Transition Words*

The writer does not provide sequence and/or transition words between sections or provides words that are so confusing the reader is unable to sort out one section from another.

The writer does not use sequence words or transitions to help the reader follow the ideas and thinking in this piece.

Scoring Guide

The paper rated these scores on a 6-point scale.

Ideas	2
ORGANIZATION	**1**
Voice	2
Word Choice	2
Sentence Fluency	2
Conventions	3

C. *Structuring the Body*

The writer does not show clearly what comes first, next, and last, making it difficult to understand how sections fit together. The writer slows down when he or she should speed up and speeds up when he or she should slow down.

This piece does not have a clear beginning, middle, or end. Instead, it's a collection of random thoughts about the dog, losing the dog, missing the dog, not missing the dog, and other details that bounce in and out of paragraphs.

D. *Ending With a Sense of Resolution*

The writer ends the piece with no conclusion at all—or nothing more than "The End" or something equally bland. There is no sense of resolution, no sense of completion.

The writer seems conflicted at the end. To what degree does he or she miss the dog? The reader ends the piece without a strong sense of wrapping up the main idea.

What We Say to the Writer

There's definitely a story to tell about your dog, JJ. Let's talk about what you want to focus on in your piece and then put your story in a logical order that will help the reader understand what you think and feel. Start by determining how you really feel about JJ. Do you miss him? How much? How was JJ different from other dogs? What was his most memorable quality? You might want to use a graphic organizer for a narrative that will help you sort out what's important from what isn't. Don't try to cover everything. Really zoom in on one major point or emotion. Then you will be able to reveal how you feel about JJ Think about beginning your piece in the middle of the action, for example, one time you and JJ were together doing something fun. Start off strong!

JJ

I was jumping up and down because it was my first time moving. JJ acted sad because it seemed like he knew we were moving. When we got rid of him he acted very sad the way his eyes were down.

When I was nine we had to get rid of my dog named JJ. We had to move. I was excited because it was my first time moving. I was moving into a house. It was my first move into a house.

I had him my whole life. I had JJ for nine years (that's a lot.) I cried my eyes out when I had to get rid of him. It felt weird without coming home to a dog.

We gave my dog to my mom's friend. I was sad when I didn't have him for a while. Then, after a while I got over it. I was very sad because it was my first dog, and you can't really let go because JJ was the best dog. He was a nice dog, most of the time, he was very playful. My brothers would torment him, like I am going to get your food, and he would growl.

I am sad he is gone. Sometimes I still think of him, and miss him. I wish I knew where he was because I want to visit him. I don't know where he is because my mom's friend gave it to her friend. I need to see him at least one more time. I am over it because I don't miss him as much as I did before.

Ideas

Organization

Voice

Word Choice

Sentence Fluency

Conventions

Analysis of the Voice Trait in "'Have you ever gotten home'"

What We See in the Writing

Phrases such as "gloriously sticky, chewy food," and "glazing you with a warm happy feeling" really sell this piece and create an unmistakable voice! The use of active verbs throughout gives the piece energy and contributes to the playful tone of the piece. Readers will no doubt notice their mouths watering. Even someone who doesn't like peanut butter may want to give it a try after reading this. This piece is an excellent example of how the word choice and voice traits can work hand in hand supporting each other beautifully. ***Voice Score:* 6, Exceptional**

A. Establishing a Tone

The writer cares about the topic, and it shows. The writing is expressive and compelling. The reader feels the writer's conviction, authority, and integrity.

Speaking directly to the reader, the writer provides a real-life scenario to which we can all relate. He or she asks questions and draws us in with lively turns of phrase and descriptive language. There is no doubt this writer is a peanut butter fan.

B. Conveying the Purpose

The writer makes clear his or her reason for creating the piece. He or she offers a point of view that is appropriate for the mode (narrative, expository, or persuasive), which compels the reader to read on.

The writer's voice is engaging and convincing. By writing so clearly about the benefits of peanut butter to relieve stress and provide good nutrition, the author probably inspired readers to drop everything and go to the kitchen in search of some peanut butter. I know I did!

C. Creating a Connection to the Audience

The writer speaks in a way that makes the reader want to listen. He or she has considered what the reader needs to know and the best way to convey it by sharing his or her fascination, feelings, and opinions about the topic.

What reader can't relate to wanting to relieve some stress after a long day at work or school? And this writer uses that universal feeling as the context for the argument about how great peanut butter is. It would be hard not to find yourself nodding at each point along the way.

D. Taking Risks to Create Voice

The writer expresses ideas in new ways, which makes the piece interesting and original. The writing sounds like the writer because of his or her use of distinctive, just-right words and phrases.

The writer's unique style shines through this piece. Delightful phrasing and the ability to relate to the reader through shared experiences give this piece a strong and credible voice—one that sticks (like peanut butter to the roof of your mouth) with you after you finish reading.

What We Say to the Writer

Hurrah for you. You made me rethink my "no peanut butter" decision (thank goodness!) with your passionate and credible arguments. Your piece worked on several levels. You extend your thinking way beyond the typical topic and typical description. It's obvious you feel strongly about this idea, and you draw upon experience to support your point of view. Connecting peanut butter to childhood bliss is masterful. You may have a future in advertising. That's certainly a place where voice makes all the difference.

Scoring Guide

The paper rated these scores on a 6-point scale.

Ideas	6
Organization	6
VOICE	**6**
Word Choice	6
Sentence Fluency	6
Conventions	5

"Have you ever gotten home"

Have you ever gotten home from a hard day of work and been bombarded with people asking you to do things, pulling at you from every directions, grasping for your attention? You just get stressed out. Well here is the one thing that can help. Forget all those fake gimmicky products like stress relieving masks, aroma therapy candles, they might leave you with a nice smelling room and a smooth face, but the stress will still be there. What you need is peanut butter.

Go into the kitchen, get the biggest sized spoon you can find, and dig into the peanut butter jar. Once you get a massive spoonfull go listen to one of your favorite songs, or watch your favorite show and lick the spoon clean. Believe me, you will feel a lot better.

Now you may have a few questions, like why peanut butter? Well, peanut butter is a gloriously sticky, chewy food so I find it the very best to relieve stress. Also it can be eaten on so many foods, apples, sandwiches, bagels, and it tastes delicious on waffles. You may think that peanut butter is too much of a fatty, unhealthy food to eat very much of it, but it is not necessarily bad for you. In fact, the type of peanut butter I recommend is all natural, made purely of peanuts, Adams All Natural Peanut Butter. If you do have a weight problem you should consider giving up some other junky, artificial foods to fit peanut butter into your diet.

I'm sure everyone has at least a few childhood memories of going to the park on a warm, sunny day, laying down in a blanket, and opening up the picnic basket to find that warm gooey peanut butter and jelly sandwich. The sunshine is beating down on your face, glazing you with a warm happy feeling like frosting on a donut, and then you take a bite. The soft bread gives way under your teeth so that you can reach the best part, what a peanut butter and jelly sandwich is all about, the peanut butter.

So believe me when that tasty peanut butter slides down your throat you'll remember those happy carefree days, and some of your stress will go with it.

Analysis of the Voice Trait in "Don't Be a Pest, Clean Up Your Mess!"

What We See in the Writing

While this piece should be revised for ideas and organization, it contains a strong sense of voice. The writer is passionate about this topic and generous in dispensing advice to classmates. This is a memorable piece for voice, even if it is a little over the top at times. ***Voice Score:* 5, Strong**

A. Establishing a Tone

The writer cares about the topic, and it shows. The writing is expressive and compelling. The reader feels the writer's conviction, authority, and integrity.

Organization is a challenge for most middle school students—sometimes it's a huge stumbling block to their success in school. This writer obviously believes he or she can help by providing motivation and personal advice. There is no question how the writer feels.

B. Conveying the Purpose

The writer makes clear his or her reason for creating the piece. He or she offers a point of view that is appropriate for the mode (narrative, expository, or persuasive), which compels the reader to read on.

It takes skill to build solid support, to address possible opposition, and to keep a respectful tone, especially for middle schoolers, who often think an argument is the same thing as a fight. But this writer uses the right tactics in this piece to create a strong persuasive piece.

> ### Scoring Guide
> *The paper rated these scores on a 6-point scale.*
>
> | | |
> |---|---|
> | Ideas | 4 |
> | Organization | 4 |
> | **VOICE** | **5** |
> | Word Choice | 4 |
> | Sentence Fluency | 5 |
> | Conventions | 4 |

C. Creating a Connection to the Audience

The writer speaks in a way that makes the reader want to listen. He or she has considered what the reader needs to know and the best way to convey it by sharing his or her fascination, feelings, and opinions about the topic.

This writer speaks personally and sincerely to the target audience, whom he or she knows well. The counterargument shows the writer has tapped into the audience's thinking and need for information to form their own opinions.

D. Taking Risks to Create Voice

The writer expresses ideas in new ways, which makes the piece interesting and original. The writing sounds like the writer because of his or her use of distinctive, just-right words and phrases.

Emphatic, passionate examples and advice create this writer's convincing tone. We get a sense of an organized—almost obsessively so—student behind this piece.

What We Say to the Writer

Good job handling a persuasive piece! You kept your audience clearly in mind as you planned each point and counterpoint. You might want to read it over for redundancy, however. If you've made the point already, it's not necessary to repeat it. Your passion for the topic shines through in every part of the piece. Strong conventions help your voice shine through, too. Conventions help the reader understand how you want the piece to flow, especially when he or she reads it aloud. There are places where you can still work on this trait, even though you already show strength in those places. In your next draft, think about how you can fine-tune conventions to make the voice in your piece even stronger.

Don't Be a Pest, Clean Up Your Mess!

"Mooooooooom, do you know where my shirt is? I've looked everywhere!"

I know that at least one time in everyone's life, they had that scared nervous feeling in their stomach when you realized that you can't seem to find something you really need. And, you also have to have it and be in the car in less than a few minutes. I know what you needed to be: you absolutely, positively needed to be organized. You should always be organized because you can have more time to do fun things with your extra time, and you don't lose things in that mess you call your closet.

Now I know that at least some people disagree with me and say that "I don't need to be organized, it takes up too much time, and besides, why does it matter as long as I can find it?" That is sooooo sad, and it's not even true!! When you take the time out of your day just to quickly tidy up your room every day, you wouldn't have to spend at least two hours out of your weekend just to clean your room. And if you take one day you're not doing anything, the best thing to do is to completely clean your room and get organized, you'll realize that it's not really as hard as you thought it was. And as for the work, there's nothing bad about being a hard worker, and as Calvin's dad says about things you don't want to do, "It builds character."

TV, video games, books, movies, crafting, & hanging out. You can do all those things and Bunches of other fun stuff because guess what? When you keep your room clean you have more time for fun things you actually want to do. Especially in school: when you are organized, you'll find that you have more time to catch up on homework, writing, reading, or the occasional favorite: sleep. (Although I would Not advise it) If you aren't organized, you tend to always be one step behind because you have to look hard for a missing paper, or you found a missing paper that you have to turn in.

When a big soccer game is only in about an hour and you need to find your jersey, no problem-o! You just need to go to your closet and take it off the hanger. When you are organized you don't lose many things and you can find them easier. For instance, when you aren't organized, you always tend to lose your homework, and then you have to dig through mounds of old graded papers. When you are organized and you keep all of your homework in your folder and you need to check a paper, all you have to do is take your checking pen, get your homework out of your folder, and check it. Of course, you're not going to never lose stuff that would just not be human! But if you don't want to lose so much stuff, you may want to get, and stay, organized.

So if you are organized, good for you, you're ahead of the game, but if you're not, I will advise you now, that you should. If you get organized, you will have more time to do fun things that are fun, and you won't lose as many things in that rat's nest of a room.

Ideas · Organization · Voice · Word Choice · Sentence Fluency · Conventions

Analysis of the Voice Trait in "GONE!!!"

What We See in the Writing

This piece is entertaining and delightful. The reader roots for this writer as he (assuming this is a male) proves to himself that he is good at baseball! The order of information is confusing in places, but the overall sense is that the writer is present in this piece and talking right to the reader. **Voice Score: 4, Refining**

A. Establishing a Tone

The writer has established a tone that can be described as "pleasing" or "sincere," but not "passionate" or "compelling." He or she attempts to create a tone that hits the mark, but the overall result feels generic.

While the writer establishes an enthusiastic tone, there are places in the piece where the description is awkward, so the writer's connection with the audience fades—for example, "But, still running hard I couldn't hear the birds chirping."

B. Conveying the Purpose

The writer has chosen a voice for the piece that is not completely clear. There are only a few moments when the reader understands where the writer is coming from and why he or she wrote the piece.

The writer shares this story because it taught him something about himself—he is good at baseball! What we'd like to know is why that is important to him and what baseball means to him.

> ### Scoring Guide
>
> *The paper rated these scores on a 6-point scale.*
>
> Ideas 4
>
> Organization 4
>
> **VOICE** **4**
>
> Word Choice 4
>
> Sentence Fluency 5
>
> Conventions 4

C. Creating a Connection to the Audience

The writer keeps the reader at a distance. The connection between reader and writer is tenuous because the writer reveals little about what is important or meaningful about the topic.

The writer is "in the moment," reveling in his success. It's enough to write a story that focuses on a special event, but the voice of this piece would be stronger if the writer could relate his experience to one the reader might have had that, though different, provided this same sense of accomplishment.

D. Taking Risks to Create Voice

The writer creates a few moments that catch the reader's attention, but only a few. The piece sounds like anyone could have written it. It lacks the energy, commitment, and conviction that would distinguish it from other pieces on the same topic.

The story seems very personal at first, but most of the details are fairly predictable. The writer relates a fairly typical sports story—I wasn't sure I could do it, but then I did and it felt great—leaving the reader wishing for a bit more individual insight.

What We Say to the Writer

This is a personal story and a unique event, yet any person who has hit a home run could share many of the same details that you write here. You've included description, but consider adding in the feelings that go along with this story; that will strengthen the voice in the piece. If you went up to bat as unsure as the introduction hints, don't be afraid to express that insecurity. It will make the home run feel much more satisfying to the reader.

GONE!!!

It was the top of the first inning. The score was 0-0 and there were no outs. One of my teammates, Mario, was up to bat. Just for a split second I looked at the bench while I was on deck. Next thing I knew, there was one out and I was next to bat. But, who would've realized that I was good at something at that moment.

Okay, recap, last game for my baseball team in the AABC World Series in New York, and there's one out. Now, I walk up to the plate hearing the chatter from the bench and the screaming fans. With every stride I can hear the hard gravel beneath my cleats. I step in, get my right foot set, and then step out of the chalk box with my left foot. I look down to my third base coach, get the sign, and take a deep breath. From there I look right into the pitchers big green eyes.

With every moment passing by, the adrenalin is killing me. I just want to hit the ball. Then, the pitcher came to a set. Looking down straight at his arm I could see the grip he had on the ball. But I couldn't exactly see what pitch he was going to throw. By the look on his face he looked like he had been punched in the gut. right then and there I saw him start to heeve the white, scarlet seamed ball.

Fastball, I quickly thought as I saw the seams rotating. With a swing that made it seem like my life depended on it, I heard the loud cry from the bat. I looked up to see a high fly ball. Chalk and dirt flew as I kicked at the ground. But, still running hard I couldn't hear the birds chirping.

I raised my arms in triumph as I saw a tiny white dot hit the cement outside of the field. GONEE!! A homerun, I couldn't believe it.

After the game not only did I realize I was good. But people were telling me I was a good baseball player. I think hitting a home run is a great way to realize you're good at something. So, yeah, I thinking I'm stickin' to baseball.

Analysis of the Voice Trait in "'I love your book'"

What We See in the Writing

Phrases such as "love your book," "also very funny," and "touched me" are reactions, but they are not terribly credible without a more personal touch by this writer. The writer tries to infuse some life into the piece with a few good examples, but overall, he or she stays on the surface of the topic, never digging in deeply enough for us to feel the real heat of his or her reaction to the book. The reader can sense what's right below the surface but is left hungry for the writer's unique way of sharing his or her reaction to the book. *Voice Score:* **3, Developing**

A. Establishing a Tone

The writer has established a tone that can be described as "pleasing" or "sincere," but not "passionate" or "compelling." He or she attempts to create a tone that hits the mark, but the overall result feels generic.

Generic statements and generic reactions make up the bulk of this piece. Yet there is an underlying feeling of the writer's genuine appreciation for the book. The writer needs to let go and express himself or herself without concern for being correct, and simply be honest.

Scoring Guide	
The paper rated these scores on a 6-point scale.	
Ideas	3
Organization	2
VOICE	**3**
Word Choice	3
Sentence Fluency	2
Conventions	3

B. Conveying the Purpose

The writer has chosen a voice for the piece that is not completely clear. There are only a few moments when the reader understands where the writer is coming from and why he or she wrote the piece.

This writer could have a strong piece if he or she developed vivid details instead of leaning on telling statements like "I love your book." Safe generalities mute moments of engagement.

C. Creating a Connection to the Audience

The writer keeps the reader at a distance. The connection between reader and writer is tenuous because the writer reveals little about what is important or meaningful about the topic.

This piece is like a limp handshake; it's not bad, but it's not good, either.

D. Taking Risks to Create Voice

The writer creates a few moments that catch the reader's attention, but only a few. The piece sounds like anyone could have written it. It lacks the energy, commitment, and conviction that would distinguish it from other pieces on the same topic.

Of the four key qualities, this is the one the writer needs to work on the most. This writer sticks with everything familiar, resulting in a safe but bland piece of writing.

What We Say to the Writer

I'm glad you liked the book. If you had written a book and a student had sent you a letter like this, what would you want to know? If it were me, I would want to understand why you loved the book and how it touched you—the emotions it sparked and the connections to your own life you made as you read it. You've danced around the surface of those emotions in your piece. You never really show the reader why you liked the book. As a reader, I want to know more. Let's find a couple of mentor texts where writers are passionate about their topics, and let's examine how they "show, not tell" so their readers feel their excitement.

Ideas

Organization

Voice

Word Choice

Sentence Fluency

Conventions

"I love your book"

I love your book *Joey Pigza Swallowed the Key.* It really helped me understand people with ADD, and other problems similar to that act the way they do. People need to read the book because some people look down on them because they don't understand. It's a shame because those people can be very good friends if you get to know them.

The book is also very funny. It addresses a serious subject while also being comical. That had to be difficult to do.

There are a couple of students like Joey in our school, so that is how I know a little about them. Sometimes they get out of hand, but most of the time they act somewhat normal. I would not want to be treated like they are because sometimes they are not given respect by everybody. It is not fair to them. I'm glad your book addressed this problem.

It reminds me of how some people think you are different because of the color of your skin. Everybody is the same no matter what your skin color is or if you have a problem like ADD or anything else. It is crazy that some people think like that. Everybody should be treated the same.

Your book *Joey Pigza Swallowed the Key* touched me and I hope it will touch many others in the future.

McLean County Unit #5
201-EJHS

Analysis of the Voice Trait in "Pops"

What We See in the Writing

This writer injects moments of raw emotion in several places, but unfortunately, we only get these few flashes. The reader senses the writer (likely male) has a good relationship with his father, even though things aren't always the best. It would be a stronger piece if he'd reveal more of what makes their time together special, why he respects his father, or even where the nickname "Pops" comes from and how he knows his father doesn't mind. **Voice Score: 2, Emerging**

A. Establishing a Tone

The writer has produced a lifeless piece—one that is monotonous, mechanical, repetitious, and/or off-putting to the reader.

Except for a few moments, such as "It's serious time," the piece is a list. The reader is left to interpret why these events are significant to the writer.

B. Conveying the Purpose

The writer chose the topic for mysterious reasons. The piece may be filled with random thoughts, technical jargon, or inappropriate vocabulary, making it impossible to discern how the writer feels about the topic.

The reader gets a limited look at the writer's purpose and feelings, especially in the last few sentences. In other parts the writer waffles back and forth, undermining the voice. For example, "Pops is usually in a gook [good] mood when I get home, but sometimes he's mad from work or something I did," leaves the reader wondering about the main point and how the reader really feels about his father's moods.

> ## Scoring Guide
> *The paper rated these scores on a 6-point scale.*
>
> Ideas 3
> Organization 1
> **VOICE** **2**
> Word Choice 2
> Sentence Fluency 2
> Conventions 2

C. Creating a Connection to the Audience

The writer provides no evidence that he or she has considered what the reader might need to know to connect with the topic. Or there is an obvious mismatch between the piece's tone and the intended audience.

This writer tried to work some thoughts and feelings about his dad into the paper, but that's where he stopped. There's no evidence he anticipated the reader's questions and tried to answer them; instead, he hid safely behind his list of activities.

D. Taking Risks to Create Voice

The writer creates no highs and lows. The piece is flat and lifeless, causing the reader to wonder why he or she wrote it in the first place. The writer's voice does not pop out, even for a moment.

The reader senses the writer wants to share his thoughts and feelings; there are hints of it in a couple of places. But he has not committed to the topic firmly enough to ensure his personal and reflective ideas come through.

What We Say to the Writer

It sounds like you and your father have some good times together. Strengthening the voice in this piece would help the reader get a better understanding of your relationship. Let's try something: Write your last sentence at the top of a piece of paper. Group the ideas you have into categories, such as "camping" and "mini-dragster." Now think about how these activities can be used to illustrate your father. What do you want us to know about your father? How do you want us to feel about your father? What memories do you have of each of these activities that relate specifically to him? Think about what details you need to use to help us understand your father the way you see him. You are in charge, and you can reveal what you wish to us. Voice is a very powerful way to show readers thoughts and ideas that are hard to put into words.

Pops

Most people think my old man is a hard worker when it comes to basic maintenance. I usually call him Pops but my mom hates it when I call him that. He doesn't care. My dad looks like me but he is a lot taller. Hopefully that won't be for too long. He has blue eye's, blonde hair. Pops is usually in a good mood when I get home, but sometimes he's mad from work or something I did. When it comes to hunting, it is not fun and games any more. It is serious time. My dad likes to go camping with all of our friends. We go tubing, fishing, and swimming. His favorite place to go is Chute. They have a lot of things to do there like go on jumping rock. There are also great fishing holes. When we are home, I enjoy working on a mini dragster we got a 15hp engine with a six speed tranny and it is about 7 ½ feet long. I had so much fun. When he would spin me around in it. That is why I love my pops because we do so much together.

Analysis of the Voice Trait in "'School uniforms'"

What We See in the Writing

By the end of the first paragraph, most readers will find their attention drifting to something else. The writer offers no compelling, interesting information, and so it's hard to connect with him or her. The piece feels forced and lifeless, an assignment, not a sincere attempt to communicate something important or interesting to the writer.

***Voice Score:* 1, Rudimentary**

A. Establishing a Tone

The writer has produced a lifeless piece—one that is monotonous, mechanical, repetitious, and/or off-putting to the reader.

This piece exists on life support, it doesn't breathe on its own. The reader doesn't feel a connection to the writer, nor does the writer seem to care much about the topic.

B. Conveying the Purpose

The writer chose the topic for mysterious reasons. The piece may be filled with random thoughts, technical jargon, or inappropriate vocabulary, making it impossible to discern how the writer feels about the topic.

It's hard to imagine this writer chose this topic because he or she didn't show any ownership of the idea. However even with an assigned topic, skilled writers can show purpose and thoughtfulness. This piece needs both.

Scoring Guide	
The paper rated these scores on a 6-point scale.	
Ideas	2
Organization	2
VOICE	**1**
Word Choice	2
Sentence Fluency	3
Conventions	3

C. Creating a Connection to the Audience

The writer provides no evidence that he or she has considered what the reader might need to know to connect with the topic. Or there is an obvious mismatch between the piece's tone and the intended audience.

Because the writer has not taken a stand, he or she is not able to connect with the audience. It's like a toaster that's not plugged in—no electricity, no toast. This piece is an example of how the ideas trait is the heart of any piece of writing, and without the heart, there is no energy.

D. Taking Risks to Create Voice

The writer creates no highs and lows. The piece is flat and lifeless, causing the reader to wonder why he or she wrote it in the first place. The writer's voice does not pop out, even for a moment.

This writer hides behind safe choices about everything from ideas to words. We never hear the person behind the writer. It seems obvious that the writer wrote this piece in order to fulfill a requirement—nothing more.

What We Say to the Writer

It would be wonderful if we could always write about what matters to us. However, sometimes we are asked to write about topics that do not appeal to us. Even if you are not passionate about a topic, giving sincere effort to making your writing clear will add voice. Let's start by revising the introduction and engaging the reader. Picture yourself wearing a uniform to school every day. Take five minutes and jot down every idea that pops into your head as you visualize—what you feel like, what you see, how your friends react, what your closet looks like . . . anything. Read over your list: were your thoughts mostly positive or mostly negative? Choose what side of this issue to write about based on your answer. Then review various leads we noted from other texts we read and discussed this year and see if anything fits and gets you going.

"School uniforms"

School uniforms are a large contraversy in the United States. Many people encourage schools to have uniforms, other people are strongly opposed to the idea. I am not sure whether I would like them or not. There are good and bad concepts about school uniforms, this paragraph will explain some of them.

A negative about wearing school uniforms is the cost. There are some families who might not be able to pay for school uniforms. Something that could happen as a result of this is that APS might have to buy uniforms for those who can't. As a result of that, the schools may not have enough money to buy other needed materials.

A good thing about school uniforms is that there might be less violence. There are gangs in areas of the United States where, if you wear "their color" you could get into trouble with that gang. Therefore, if people don't get into trouble with gangs there wouldn't be as many shootings, stabbings, et cetera, which proves that there are good and bad concepts about uniforms.

Analysis of the Word Choice Trait in "Reasons to Appreciate the Arts"

What We See in the Writing

The writer uses words to create the argument that we need the arts to strengthen and support our culture. "Every facet of humanity's jewel is lit by the arts" is a metaphor that extends through the piece, each line rife with vivid verbs, specific nouns, and adjectives that create a scene for readers to fall into. And fall we do, with phrases such as "Colorful billboards rise before us, cars with flawless design glide by us, music flows into our ears" that light up the piece from beginning to end.

***Word Choice Score:* 6, Exceptional**

A. Applying Strong Verbs

The writer uses many "action words," giving the piece punch and pizzazz. He or she has stretched to find lively verbs that add energy to the piece.

The writer used vivid verbs such as shuffled, survived, lit, drained, enlighten *to add power to the piece. The verbs are specific and energized.*

B. Selecting Striking Words and Phrases

The writer uses many finely honed words and phrases. His or her creative and effective use of literary techniques such as alliteration, simile, and metaphor makes the piece a pleasure to read.

> ### Scoring Guide
> *The paper rated these scores on a 6-point scale.*
>
> Ideas 6
>
> Organization 6
>
> Voice 6
>
> **WORD CHOICE** **6**
>
> Sentence Fluency 6
>
> Conventions 6

The writer chose words and phrases to match the purpose. For example, "We hear a rhythm and clamor, watch a play and laugh, see a monument and be stricken by awe" draws upon the senses and into the idea. And "Our world is like a painting colored by music and the arts" is a simile that helps readers develop new levels of understanding.

C. Using Specific and Accurate Words

The writer uses words with precision. He or she selects words the reader needs to fully understand the message. The writer chooses nouns, adjectives, adverbs, and so forth that create clarity and bring the topic to life.

Using a brilliantly descriptive vocabulary, this writer selects images and phrasing that work particularly well, such as the references to music and light.

D. Choosing Words That Deepen Meaning

The writer uses words to capture the reader's imagination and enhance the piece's meaning. There is a deliberate attempt to choose the best word over the first word that comes to mind.

At every point in this piece, the writer chooses words to help the reader see and feel the value of the arts. This facility with language is not first-draft material. The careful attention to imagery and use of active verbs points to revision with word choice in mind.

What We Say to the Writer

You've stated your position clearly and built a passionate argument for what you believe. There's no confusion for the reader where you stand on the arts! And you've done so lyrically and with beautiful—musical—use of language. However, have you considered any of the reasons others might not agree with you? For example, what if someone says, "Sure, the arts are important. But if you have to cut something, it should be the arts because it's not as important as learning how to read or do math." What would you say to this person? You might take the wind out of this person's argument by using the same clear thinking and powerful word choice you demonstrate here.

Reasons to Appreciate the Arts

A man shuffles through a street as dark and gray as night. There is no light in his eye, nor has there ever been. Walls glare at him, as unfeeling and mindless as the man himself. Dirt cakes the scene in a layer repulsive to the eye. Can the man love or appreciate? Or has his world without color or flavor seeped into his mind, destroying his emotions with the single, monotonous noise called apathy . . .

Humankind needs art. Our very feelings survive because of those displayed about us. Art is a language; we never speak, but we all understand it. It does not mater whether the art is music, drama, or sculpture. Even colors in a bedroom can please or minds. Like a voice, art describes, enlightens, excites, and comforts. We hear a rhythm and clamor, watch a play and laugh, see a monument and be stricken by awe. Our world is like a painting colored by music and the arts.

Every facet of humanity's jewel is lit by art. Colorful billboards rise before us, cars with flawless design glide by us, music flows into our ears. If we watch closely, we will see before us tiny but noticeable lights behind them, surrounding us and livening our souls. We know these lights by the name of culture. It illuminates our people and unveils the colors in our lives. There is but one fuel, one power that controls its entire existence: art. Since the dawn of mankind, we have drummed and painted as a part of life. Our music, our clothes, and our surroundings all bring about our culture. We depend on art for the culture by which we thrive.

There are a few places where culture and art are harder to express, however. In prisons, asylums, and tyrannies, art is nearly annihilated. Gone with it is all the freedom of our mind and soul. The man in the empty street is a prisoner; of man or tyrant I do not know. His thoughts have been drained in the gray of the world, and as a prisoner he cannot enjoy his world or believe personal beliefs. Because of this numbness of mind, any force can overtake him and possess him with its own will. Art is freedom; when it leaves the world, so will the minds of every man, woman, and child.

The arts are part of our lives. It creates emotions we can feel and share, and it powers culture so our souls can survive. More importantly, though, art grants us freedom. We must appreciate art because it is the foundation of humanity.

Analysis of the Word Choice Trait in "Midnight's Christmas"

What We See in the Writing

What an interesting piece. The core storyline is good—some room for improvement—and overall it's solid. With the addition of the section toward the end that shows what is happening to Midnight, the dog, the piece takes the reader to a whole new level. Here the writer stretches for imagery and description, using strong verbs and "just right" words and phrases, drawing the reader into a new perspective—that of the dog. The words in the piece are strongest in that intriguing part of the story.
Word Choice Score: 5, Strong

A. Applying Strong Verbs

The writer uses many "action words," giving the piece punch and pizzazz. He or she has stretched to find lively verbs that add energy to the piece.

In addition to creating imagery, this writer uses strong verbs to evoke emotion. The reader understands Luna's moods through words like coddled, mumbled, jerked, *and* collapsed.

B. Selecting Striking Words and Phrases

The writer uses many finely honed words and phrases. His or her creative and effective use of literary techniques such as alliteration, simile, and metaphor makes the piece a pleasure to read.

Any dog lover will connect with phrases such as "the dog's soft fur acting as a comfort" and "Midnight leaped into her arms and she collapsed, laughing and cuddling her puppy." While it may be a bit dramatic, the section about the dog's plight will capture both the hearts and imaginations of readers.

> ## Scoring Guide
> *The paper rated these scores on a 6-point scale.*
>
> | | |
> |---|---|
> | Ideas | 4 |
> | Organization | 4 |
> | Voice | 4 |
> | **WORD CHOICE** | **5** |
> | Sentence Fluency | 5 |
> | Conventions | 5 |

C. Using Specific and Accurate Words

The writer uses words with precision. He or she selects words the reader needs to fully understand the message. The writer chooses nouns, adjectives, adverbs, and so forth that create clarity and bring the topic to life.

Besides strong verbs and adjectives, the writer takes a risk by changing the tense from past to present to contrast the dog's story with the girl's. This is a clever choice by the writer—it shows maturity in using language effectively.

D. Choosing Words That Deepen Meaning

The writer uses words to capture the reader's imagination and enhance the piece's meaning. There is a deliberate attempt to choose the best word over the first word that comes to mind.

Middle schoolers feel emotions deeply . . . and quickly. By embedding strong words in short, sometimes jerky passages, the writer helps us visualize the story and understand the young character.

What We Say to the Writer

You have a talent for creating imagery and helping readers visualize the topic. You used the right verbs to show the puppy's movements and to contrast Luna's feelings about moving with her mother's feelings. You also take a big risk by changing the verb tense in the dog's section. I wanted to know more in a couple of places, such as the section between the mom's announcement and the picture's flying out the window. Let's talk through that part and see if you can help your readers fill in the blanks.

Midnight's Christmas

Luna cuddled her black lab against her chest, the dog's soft fur acting as a comfort while she cried.

She had just lost her grandma—one of the people she was closest to. Her heart was aching and the only comfort she had left was her little puppy, Midnight.

"I'm home!" called her mom and Luna jerked; Midnight pounced on the floor, tail wagging.

"Hi mom." said Luna grimly.

"Hi! Guess what, Luna?" asked her mom excitedly.

"Hmm?"

"We're moving! Your father just bought a beautiful house with three bedrooms so you and your sister won't have to share one!"

"Great." mumbled Luna, sitting down again. That was the last thing she wanted. Now she would have to leave behind her grandpa and all of her friends!

"And the best part is that we're moving in a week!" squealed her mom.

A week came by faster than Luna expected, and soon she was in the car with her sister and Midnight (who was on her lap).

Luna was looking at a photo of her grandma with the window open. With one last look at her old house, the car started and they were on their way.

The house was very far away, and about 2 hours into the trip, the photo flew out the window.

"Aaaaaah!" No!" screamed Luna. "My picture!"

Without a moment to spare, Midnight jumped out of the window and bounded down the road after the photo.

"Don't worry, she'll sniff her way back."

"The picture can't have gone too far. She'll be back before you know it."

The words of comfort did nothing to help. 3, 4, 5 weeks passed and Midnight never came.

She didn't know what to think. She'd lost her grandma, her dog, what next?

Christmas came and Midnight still never showed up. Poor Luna. She sat by the window, looking for a trace of black against the sparkly white blanket of snow.

A black dog as dark as night moves slowly, staggering across the glittering snow. But that is not the only thing shining. Millions of light bulbs flash red and green against the dark winter sky. The dog collapses, unable to move anymore. The snow does not seem cold to her, for she is immersed by memories of many years ago . . . A single tear trickles down into her black fur, and then she is still, snow drifting from above, covering the dog with a fluffy white blanket . . . Then she is lifted by warm hands, and she hears the tinkle of a bell. She opens her eyes and an old man with a pink nose and a beard as white as snow looks down at her with kind, twinkling eyes. She blinks, and the man is gone. Filled with newfound strength, she runs for a long, long time. Her black fur flaked with tiny snowflakes, she reaches the house.

Luna looked out the window again and saw a dog, black as night, tearing toward the house.

"Midnight!" she screamed, and flung her self out the front door, not caring that she was in her pajamas and slippers.

Midnight leaped into her arms and she collapsed, laughing and cuddling her puppy.

Snow fell on them, and right then, Luna didn't care about the presents under the tree. Midnight was the best Christmas present ever.

Analysis of the Word Choice Trait in "'Movies are like giant vats'"

What We See in the Writing

While the stew metaphor is clever, there are plenty of places in the piece where the writer relies on typical, safe words and phrases rather than those that would add the right degree of spice. Mixed in with the clear, competent explanations and descriptions are sections that are confusing. The writer needs to pay some attention to repetition as well. **Word Choice Score: 4, Refining**

A. Applying Strong Verbs

The writer uses the passive voice quite a bit and includes few "action words" to give the piece energy.

Parts of the piece, such as the second paragraph, in which the writer uses darts *and* terrorizes, *contain strong verbs, but a close look at the first paragraph reveals sentences made of "to be" verbs, many of which could become more specific and active in the next draft.*

B. Selecting Striking Words and Phrases

The writer provides little evidence that he or she has stretched for the best words or phrases. He or she may have attempted literary techniques, but they are trite or cliché for the most part.

Connecting the parts of the essay by comparing them to ingredients in a stew creates an interesting metaphor, but the writer has trouble sustaining it, falling back on overly familiar, bland words again and again.

> ### Scoring Guide
> *The paper rated these scores on a 6-point scale.*
>
> Ideas 5
> Organization 5
> Voice 5
> **WORD CHOICE 4**
> Sentence Fluency 4
> Conventions 5

C. Using Specific and Accurate Words

The writer presents specific and accurate words, except for a few related to sophisticated and/or content-related topics. Technical or irrelevant jargon is off-putting to the reader. The words rarely capture the reader's imagination.

There are a few vivid images, such as "shooting continuous volleys of spitballs." The writer accurately describes the main character's actions, and anyone who has seen the movie will appreciate this writer's descriptions, even if the words are fairly ordinary in many places.

D. Choosing Words That Deepen Meaning

The writer uses words to capture the reader's imagination and enhance the piece's meaning. There is a deliberate attempt to choose the best word over the first word that comes to mind.

The writer begins with an imaginative vat of stew, which captures the reader's attention and helps to develop the writer's analysis of the movie's aspects. It's visual and it works. Unfortunately, that attention to specificity with words is not sustained throughout.

What We Say to the Writer

You locked me in with your vat of stew metaphor. It's easy to see that words intrigue you, and I get the sense you appreciate the value of selecting the best words for your writing. Perhaps you need time to revise for the word choice trait only; don't worry about any other trait as you go back through your piece. Let's begin by underlining the verbs in the first paragraph. See if you can change at least half of the "be" verbs into action verbs. Now continue marking the verbs in the rest of the paper. Do you see other places you could revise the verbs? Look also for phrases that tell us the point rather than show us. See if you can revise sentences like "This character is really weird." I bet you can be far more descriptive of what you had in mind than *weird*.

"Movies are like giant vats"

Movies are like giant vats of stew. In order to make a really good stew, you must put a lot of different things in it. For example, vegetable stew has carrots, potatoes, and an occasional broccoli stalk along with an assortment of other things. Movies have to have a lot of ingredients to make them good as well. There are plenty of great "movie stews" out there but there are distinctly good ones. By this I'm talking about Ace Ventura: Pet Detective. This movie has all the essential ingredients in it; it has to have some kind of immaturity, a good plot, and distinct characters that you will remember forever.

There is a lot of the immaturity ingredients in this stew. For example, the main character lives in a temple that has one thousand steps. He tries to get a slinky to go down every step and it stops on the last step. Then he darts back up to try it again. Another example of when his immaturity shows is when he terrorizes an Indian who has to balance on a pole for three days. He does this by shooting continuous volleys of spitballs at him and violently shaking the pole yelling, "Earthquake test!"

Every movie needs a good plot and this one, as mature as it takes the gold. The main character is on a mission to find the Sacred Bat of two Indian clans. If he doesn't, they will go to war and annihilate each other. Little does he know the person who hired him stole the bat! He ends up getting the bat from him and barely makes it back in time. He arrived just before the two Indian armies where about to clash and ran through with the bat hollering at the top of his lungs, "Shikaka!" The word makes the Indians bow down because it is the name of the Sacred Bat.

Charcaters are the main "ingredient" that makes a movie. This character is realy weird! He arrives at a formal dinner party and took an assortment of food and arranged it on his face. He had hisparagus in teeth, cucumbers in his eyes, and baby tomatoes in his nose. Then, when he was being briefed for his mission, he started making finger puppets in front of the projector, and then, using the finger puppets, attacked the people on the slide.

No matter how you like your stew, Ace Venture: Pet Detective will fill you up and you will want to watch it again and again. No matter how many times you watch it, it is still as hilarious as the first time. This is because it has all the essentials in a movie to make it such a great movie.

Analysis of the Word Choice Trait in "Do not try this at home!"

What We See in the Writing

The writer has a good basic storyline but fails to get everything in his or her head on the paper. We get the outline, not the colored-in version. "There were big and thick branches and small and thin branches, they were all rough and some were smooth but they were really easy to climb" is an example of the writer trying to describe but coming up short. The reader gets the general idea here, but what's missing are the verbs and specific words and phrases that would bring this story into focus.

Word Choice Score: 3, Developing

A. Applying Strong Verbs

The writer uses the passive voice quite a bit and includes few "action words" to give the piece energy.

The writer leans on the passive voice and obvious words and phrases throughout. Lines such as "The funny thing is, is that ever since I broke it, I've been able to run even faster and I take that as an advantage" don't pack the same punch as those with more active verbs.

B. Selecting Striking Words and Phrases

The writer provides little evidence that he or she has stretched for the best words or phrases. He or she may have attempted literary techniques, but they are trite or cliché for the most part.

Some words just don't work, such as bogus in the sentence "My first step went bogus." Or "He says today that I had blood all over my mouth and I looked kind of funny just acting perfectly fine for a girl who just fell out of a tree." Many phrases and sentences are just a little off.

C. Using Specific and Accurate Words

The writer presents specific and accurate words, except for a few related to sophisticated and/or content-related topics. Technical or irrelevant jargon is off-putting to the reader. The words rarely capture the reader's imagination.

Phrases such as "I got really bored" and "they screamed really loud" are appropriate but not creative, vivid, or fresh.

D. Choosing Words That Deepen Meaning

The writer fills the piece with unoriginal language rather than language that results from careful revision. The words communicate the basic idea, but they are ordinary and uninspired.

The writer tries to inject some humor into the story in the first and last paragraphs of the piece, but the words do not create the irony the writer intends.

Scoring Guide

The paper rated these scores on a 6-point scale.

Ideas	3
Organization	3
Voice	4
WORD CHOICE	**3**
Sentence Fluency	3
Conventions	4

What We Say to the Writer

There is a story worth telling here, without question. The right details expressed with strong word choices will take this piece to the next level. Let's comb over your paper looking for ordinary, simple details, the ones anyone could write even if they hadn't experienced this event personally. Why don't you underline them with a colored pencil? Now let's go back through each section to add, change, or delete the phrases you found, replacing them with more colorful, interesting wording. Next, think about the important details you left out. If you need help deciding, read your piece out loud to a friend. Pause at the end of each paragraph to ask if he or she has questions or needs details to visualize the passage. Make notes of what you see in your mind as you explain. List the words and phrases that capture the moments or images best, then go back and see if you can work them into the story.

Do not try this at home!

This story is very, quite interesting but, before you read it I have some advice; first, don't ever, ever climb trees to high to where you can't get down and second listen to your friends at all times! Got it? Good!

Ok , so it was the second to last day of school. My friends, Carrie, Abbie and I were all in Carrie's back yard and while they were searching through my cell phone I got really bored so I went to the far back to climb the 30ft tree (I wasn't planning on climbing that high though). There were big and thick branches and small and thin branches, they were all rough and some were smooth but they were really easy to climb. I climbed about 20 branches, as my friends yelled and screamed for me to get down my stubborn self I didn't listen and I kept on climbing.

I kept on climbing until I was about 15 maybe 18 feet up in that tree. As I saw how high, my breath dropped. I wanted to just climb down but my conscience wouldn't let me. But I decided to just face my fear and go for it. My first step was bogus. One step, SLIP! And I flew down to the ground from 18 feet in the air! My friends claim that they screamed really loud, which isn't to hard to believe because they thought I was dead. As Carrie sprinted up the street to my house I just lay there peacefully and all of the neighborhood kids ran down the street to see me.

When I woke up the first time I asked if I could get up because I felt perfectly fine. Of course Carrie's dad said no. I turned my head and just said hi to my friend Brian and he waved but was looking at me very strange. He says today that I had blood all over my mouth and I looked kind of funny just acting perfectly fine for a girl who just fell out of a tree. Then I guess I passed out again. (Hint that I don't remember any of this happening because I had a concussion and all of my friends told me this story over and over again).

When my mom came down to Carrie's house, I tried to walk to the car and then the worst pain in my life hit me. The cold stab of shock and pain and the world was spinning faster and faster each moment. Everything hurt so badly when I got in the car. When I got to the hospital they immediately got me into a room and then rushed me to the X-ray room. As the doctor walked into the room, he picked up the X-rays and he said just a minor concussion. This is not too bad from falling 18 feet out of a tree. But then he said it.

My first broken bone from falling out of a tree, story of my life. One of the hardest things to brake in your body is your pelvis. I get the stupidest stunt award from my friends and family because I broke that exact bone! After that they just gave me some medicine which made me really loopy.

The experience changed me so much and I regret the fact that I actually climbed to 18 feet in the air and fell smack dab on by butt! The funny thing is, is that ever since I broke it, I've been able to run even faster and I take that as an advantage. My friends till make fun of me and I just have to laugh along! I'm just lucky that I didn't climb higher than I really did!

To this exact day I still go over to Carrie's house and look up into that tree and wonder "how in the world did I get that high, fall, and not die?" I guess im just a lucky person. But make sure you listen to my advice and listen to what your friends say and don't ever climb trees if you have a really good chance that you can fall out and break your pelvis like I did! But you have to admit that I fell out of a tree and basically broke my butt? Am I right?

Analysis of the Word Choice Trait in "'To the editor'"

What We See in the Writing

This writer sticks with what is safe—in the structure, with the examples, and with the word choice. The introduction and conclusion are rudimentary at best, and the piece reads more like a first draft than a final, polished piece. This writer needs to brainstorm words and phrases that work with the topic and add them on the next draft, substituting overused words for more original and interesting ones. Essays demand tight writing; excellent word choice is how readers understand the specifics of what the writer is trying to explain. This piece communicates only in a general way.

Word Choice Score: 2, Emerging

A. Applying Strong Verbs

The writer makes no attempt to select verbs with energy. The passive voice dominates the piece.

Might be, could be, will, have, are litter the piece. Texting is a new verb, and it works, but is used repetitively. The result is low energy from beginning to end.

B. Selecting Striking Words and Phrases

The writer uses words that are repetitive, vague, and/or unimaginative. Limited meaning comes through because the words are so lifeless.

There's little attempt to engage the reader with words in this piece. The word kids begins the first three paragraphs, followed by people in the fourth paragraph. Vague.

> **Scoring Guide**
>
> *The paper rated these scores on a 6-point scale.*
>
> Ideas 2
> Organization 2
> Voice 2
> **WORD CHOICE** **2**
> Sentence Fluency 2
> Conventions 4

C. Using Specific and Accurate Words

The writer misuses words, making it difficult to understand what he or she is conveying. Or he or she uses words that are so technical, inappropriate, or irrelevant that the average reader can hardly understand what he or she is saying.

Most of the words are specific to the topic, and with the exception of a few that are mixed up, most words are used appropriately. Unfortunately, this writer makes no attempt to enliven the piece with a few well-placed, unique phrases.

D. Choosing Words That Deepen Meaning

The writer uses many words and phrases that simply do not work. Little meaning comes through because the language is so imprecise and distracting.

Readers understand, but only in the most general way. There is nothing new in this piece to make the reader sit up and pay attention; it would be easy to drift away while reading.

What We Say to the Writer

You have chosen a hot topic; now it's time to make your word choices sizzle! Your introduction sets the tone, so that would be the place to snag the reader. How better to do this than by using words creatively and effectively? What about starting with a scenario? You could use your personal experience with your friend who texted all night. I'll bet lots of kids, and maybe some adults, can relate to that story. Use words and phrases that put us right in the middle of that situation, re-creating it so vividly we feel we are there with you. Draw on your senses.

"To the editor"

To the editor:

Kids with cell phones text too much.

Kids are texting instead of doing homework or other things. Therefore, the amount of kids doing outside activities is low. Also, kids might be tired in class because they could have been texting all night.

Kids will loose their person to person communication skills because they will just be sending text messages all the time. They won't have anything to talk about, because they would just text each other. Also, it is easier to write stuff to others and hide behind your words than to talk face to face.

People may lose relationships with their family, because they are texting all the time. Also, your parents might tell you not to text but you do it behind their back. You could be spreading rumors about your friends in text messages. Once my friend came over to my house, and the whole time she was texting, so we didn't get to spend much time with each other.

Do you feel the same way I do?

Ideas

Organization

Voice

Word Choice

Sentence Fluency

Conventions

Analysis of the Word Choice Trait in "Ngaka Maseko High"

What We See in the Writing

From the first sentence, the reader wonders who "they" and "we" are. Where is this taking place? Are we in the past or present? It's a classic middle school mistake that creates confusion—pronouns without antecedents. The lack of information and vague words distract the reader and create a barrier to understanding.

***Word Choice Score:* 1, Rudimentary**

A. Applying Strong Verbs

The writer makes no attempt to select verbs with energy. The passive voice dominates the piece.

Several sentences simply focus on what one group has and the other does not. The writer chooses simple verbs such as live *and* paint *The verbs do not show action or change, which would add energy to the writing.*

B. Selecting Striking Words and Phrases

The writer uses words that are repetitive, vague, and/or unimaginative. Limited meaning comes through because the words are so lifeless.

The writer gives limited information using a limited vocabulary. The writer needs to be reminded of how to use readily available word resources: word walls, personal word lists, thesauruses, and other reference materials in the classroom.

> ### Scoring Guide
> *The paper rated these scores on a 6-point scale.*
>
> Ideas 1
> Organization 1
> Voice 1
> **WORD CHOICE** **1**
> Sentence Fluency 1
> Conventions 2

C. Using Specific and Accurate Words

The writer misuses words, making it difficult to understand what he or she is conveying. Or he or she uses words that are so technical, inappropriate, or irrelevant the average reader can hardly understand what he or she is saying.

Because the writer leans on pronouns, we have no idea who he or she is discussing. The other words give us a vague idea of what the writer is trying to say, but that's all we get—cloudy images.

D. Choosing Words That Deepen Meaning

The writer uses many words and phrases that simply do not work. Little meaning comes through because the language is so imprecise and distracting.

The writer did not approach the piece from the reader's perspective. Once he or she reads it aloud to a peer, the writer should realize how confusing this piece is to the reader.

What We Say to the Writer

I don't have enough information yet to understand where you are going with this piece. Let's start by figuring out who the people are and name them. Then tell me exactly why you want to compare these two groups. Once you have clarified your purpose, make two lists, one for "they" and one for "we." Jot down words and phrases that come to mind for each column, but go beyond "round houses." Think about details. What color are they? Why is the structure round? Just keep going, and don't edit as you brainstorm. Before you revise, do one more thing: picture your reader as a person who has no knowledge of your topic. Think about what he or she needs to know to understand what you know. Just remember, you are the expert, and your job is to pass on your knowledge and ideas using the words and phrases that make the meaning clear.

Ngaka Maseko High

They live in round houses and we do not. The lakes have salt in them and ours does not. They paint designs on their houses and we do not. They have walls with holes in them so they can defend themselves. We do not have traditional dances either. We do dnot have villages.

Analysis of the Sentence Fluency Trait in "'It was a casual spring evening'"

What We See in the Writing

When this piece is read aloud, it's easy to hear and feel this writer's fluency. That flow grabs readers and sucks them into the writing. The writer has a mature, instinctive sense of phrasing and how to use sentence structures to further the story. The flow is smooth and easy on the ear, making it a pleasure to read, from beginning to end.

Sentence Fluency Score: 6, Exceptional

A. Crafting Well-Built Sentences

The writer carefully and creatively constructs sentences for maximum impact. Transition words such as *but, and,* and *so* are used successfully to join sentences and sentence parts.

This piece begs to be read aloud. The writer uses the sentence lengths and styles to help convey meaning, such as pairing the simple "Everything was calm and peaceful" with the longer, more detailed sentence that comes before it. The writer's control over sentences shows confidence and skill.

B. Varying Sentence Types

The writer uses various types of sentences (simple, compound, and/or complex) to enhance the central theme or storyline. The piece is made up of an effective mix of long, complex sentences and short, simple ones.

The writer uses a variety of sentence types for different purposes. For example, she uses short, direct statements to emphasize emotion. The best examples of this are toward the end, when the main character realizes the gravity of the situation. In one place, she simply states, "I started to cry," and she ends with the ever-effective "I love you, too."

> ### Scoring Guide
> *The paper rated these scores on a 6-point scale.*
>
> | | |
> |---|---|
> | Ideas | 5 |
> | Organization | 5 |
> | Voice | 5 |
> | Word Choice | 5 |
> | **SENTENCE FLUENCY** | **6** |
> | Conventions | 6 |

C. Capturing Smooth and Rhythmic Flow

The writer thinks about how the sentences sound. He or she uses phrasing that is almost musical. If the piece were read aloud, it would be easy on the ear.

The entire piece fits together seamlessly, making reading it aloud easy. When the sentences work this well, they help to underscore the meaning of the piece. Readers are free to consider what is being said rather than being distracted by awkward constructions or repetitious patterns.

D. Breaking the "Rules" to Create Fluency

The writer diverges from standard English to create interest and impact. For example, he or she may use a sentence fragment, such as "All alone in the forest." or a single word, such as "Bam!" to accent a particular moment or action. He or she might begin with informal words such as *well, and,* or *but* to create a conversational tone, or he or she might break rules intentionally to make dialogue sound authentic.

The writer sticks with standard English throughout the piece, but the choice is effective, not simply "right." The use of dialogue is natural and appropriate.

What We Say to the Writer

As I read your piece, I totally forgot where I was and got into the moment with you. Trust me, that does not happen often. Your command of sentences shows you are a master storyteller, and my guess is you are a reader, too. There are natural rhythm and tempo to this piece. I especially liked the way you avoided sentimentalizing the end. What's next? I'm looking forward to reading more of your work as you stretch into new modes and formats.

"It was a casual spring evening"

It was a casual spring evening at my family's farm. The sun was just about to set, birds were chirping with new songs and grass was more than a slight fringe. Everything was calm and peaceful.

However, an eerie feeling nagged at me; I had a strong sensation I shouldn't mount my red chestnut Missouri Foxtrotting Hourse, Elmo. I couldn't see any rational reason not to ride, so I ignored my inner voice and boosted myself up.

"Up you go, Meg" my red-headed Aunt Amy said, hoisting up my little 3-year-old sister onto our black Tennessee Walking Horse, Boo. "Are you guys ready?" my aunt said taking Bobo's lead rope.

"Yeah!" Meg piped enthusiastically.

"Yep," I said. "I'll go first."

I rode beyond the gate to the corral and turned north; Aunt Amy and Meg were not too far behind. We were going downhill on the long, gravel road when Elmo stopped. He looked around, his big brown eyes wide with some invisible fear.

"You're all right, bud," I said calmly. "There's nothing to be afraid of. Walk on." I nudged him with my heels and he walked forward.

We were passing by a little cluster of trees when a huge uproar of birds sounded from it, startling both of the horses. Elmo jumped to the right and bolted forward I kept my seat and pulled him back to a walk and turned around. I looked back at Aunt Amy and Meg.

Boo was taking off back up the road and Meg was sitting on the side of the road crying. Aunt Amy was cut at her left eyebrow, and a stream of blood was winding down the side of her freckled face. I trotted back to them.

"Are you guys okay?" I asked.

"I . . . got cut . . . by Boo's bridle," Aunt Amy said, "and Meg . . . got thrown off." I looked at Meg; she seemed traumatized, but she wasn't really injured except for a few bumps and bruises.

We quickly made our way back to the corral to put the horses away in their paddock. Then we climbed into my aunt's white truck. Meg sat on my lap, whimpering slightly as Aunt Amy drove down the hilly trail. When we reached the clearing where my dad and uncle were, we got out of the truck.

Aunt Amy explained her cut to dad and my uncle. Then my uncle drove her to the nearest hospital.

Meg and I sat on my dad's ATV and hugged each other tight. I started to cry. I cried because I knew I could have lost her. She was riding a spooky horse on gravel road with no stirrups or a helmet. If she fell on her head, she could have been killed.

So I held her close and told her, "I love you, sis."

"I love you, too."

Analysis of the Sentence Fluency Trait in "A Cry to Remember"

What We See in the Writing

The writer's raw insecurities flow throughout the piece. She slows down in sentences such as "I was only thinking about the knots in my stomach and the soon to be tears running down my cheeks" and then speeds up with short sentences as her tension increases. There are some nice moments, such as "I could feel the excitement in the room as if it was about to explode from their bodies. Why couldn't I feel this way too? Suddenly, I tasted my salty tears running down my face," interspersed with a few sentences that need rewording or reordering to be as effective.
Sentence Fluency Score: 5, Strong

A. Crafting Well-Built Sentences

The writer carefully and creatively constructs sentences for maximum impact. Transition words such as *but, and,* and *so* are used successfully to join sentences and sentence parts.

We can "hear" the writer speaking as we read because she has created a smooth, authentic piece. The transitions serve their purpose without feeling obvious to the reader. The casual way the sentence begins, "But, for once I was not thinking about how I looked; I was only thinking about the knots in my stomach and the soon to be tears running down my cheeks," is complemented with the more formal use of the semicolon.

> ## Scoring Guide
> *The paper rated these scores on a 6-point scale.*
>
> | | |
> |---|---|
> | Ideas | 5 |
> | Organization | 5 |
> | Voice | 5 |
> | Word Choice | 4 |
> | **SENTENCE FLUENCY** | **5** |
> | Conventions | 5 |

B. Varying Sentence Types

The writer uses various types of sentences (simple, compound, and/or complex) to enhance the central theme or storyline. The piece is made up of an effective mix of long, complex sentences and short, simple ones.

Short, simple statements in several places show the writer's agitation. Longer sentences of various structures contrast and create images for the reader.

C. Capturing Smooth and Rhythmic Flow

The writer thinks about how the sentences sound. He or she uses phrasing that is almost musical. If the piece were read aloud, it would be easy on the ear.

It is easy to travel with this writer through her first day of school. The sentences blend together, begging to be read aloud, one after the other.

D. Breaking the "Rules" to Create Fluency

The writer diverges from standard English to create interest and impact. For example, he or she may use a sentence fragment, such as "All alone in the forest." or a single word, such as "Bam!" to accent a particular moment or action. He or she might begin with informal words such as *well, and,* or *but* to create a conversational tone, or he or she might break rules intentionally to make dialogue sound authentic.

This writer uses fragments to help create an authentic teenage voice. It's obvious this writer cares more about the fluency of the piece than adhering to the rules.

What We Say to the Writer

When your story really gets going, the sentences flow smoothly. I could picture you moving through the halls, feeling what you described. I like the way you used short sentences to express tension in the beginning of the fourth paragraph. Keep working on "showing, not telling," and let your fluency help you with that. Why don't you go back to the beginning of the piece and see if there are places where you can create that same sense of flow? Read your piece aloud and you'll hear the difference between the first sentences and those that come later on. Think about varying the length by adding a short, declarative sentence for emphasis.

A Cry to Remember

Ugghh, that day! I remember it like a person remembers a nightmare they've had for years. It was the first day of sixth grade, and I was so terrified that you could see small droplets of sweat running down my forehead.

My family and I had just moved into a new house over the summer. It seemed as if everything was new, (the car, house, neighbors, and the new school). I hated new things. Why was so much change happening to me?

My mom took me to school on the very first day of sixth grade. It was a wet, cloudy morning, and I was extremely nervous! I remember that I was wearing a brand new outfit to go with my stylish pair of brown, sequence flats. My honey colored hair was flowing down past my shoulders. But, for once I was not thinking about how I looked; I was only thinking about the knots in my stomach and the soon to be tears running down my cheeks.

It was time; I had stalled long enough. The bell rang. Oh, how I hated that bell. I was not ready to leave yet. "Just five more minutes," I thought to myself. "I have to go take your brother to school. So hurry up and get out of the car. You'll be fine! I love you. Have a wonderful day!" Those were the last words I heard from my "way to happy" mother that morning, as I slammed the car door shut. I can't believe she was making me go through this! Didn't she care about her darling daughter? No, she only cared about her brand new oversized kitchen! As I walked into the front hallway of the middle school I could feel the happiness of everyone around me. They knew where they were going and who they were going to hangout with. I could feel the excitement in the room as if it was about to explode from their bodies. Why couldn't I feel this way too? Suddenly, I tasted my salty tears running down my face. I tried to stop them but they kept sprinting down. Down, like water shooting out after a dam bursts. "No, no, no, I can not cry on the first day of school." I thought to myself.

I quickly wiped them away as I observed the school; after all I was going to be here for three years. Three, long years! Everything looked so gigantic and overwhelming. Kids were running all over the place, trying to talk to as many of their friends as possible.

The first three hours were horrible. No one even made an effort to come up and talk to me. No one, except for a girl named Regan. I knew from the moment I saw her I was going to try my best to become her friend. The rest of the day went by fast. By the end of it I had made three more friends and planned to sit with them at lunch the next day.

A few months later everything was according to plan; I had made more friends and was a lot happier. It just took me a while to understand that not everything new is bad. Actually most of it isn't. You just have to walk into something looking for the positives. I finally forgave my mom about the whole moving situation and realized she just wanted the best for our family. I will never forget my first day of sixth grade, the huge cry I had at the beginning of the day, the knots in my stomach from my nervousness, and the new friends I made. I now understand that not everything about a new school is bad.

Analysis of the Sentence Fluency Trait in "'Have you heard of Anne Frank?'"

What We See in the Writing

There is a lot going right in this piece. However, some awkwardly constructed sentences distract the reader and break up the rhythm and flow. In a few places, the writer switches up the tempo effectively, such as "You can't get much more normal than that." In others, however, the passive voice construction and clumsy wording make reading more difficult. The writer shows sentence sense but needs to revise with sentences in mind to have a more controlled piece.

***Sentence Fluency Score:* 4, Refining**

A. Crafting Well-Built Sentences

The writer offers simple sentences that are sound, but no long, complex sentences. He or she attempts to vary the beginnings and lengths of sentences.

Thoughtful effort to construct sturdy sentences is visible in many sections. The writer is especially effective in interspersing short, simple sentences for dramatic effect.

B. Varying Sentence Types

The writer exhibits basic sentence sense and offers some sentence variety. He or she attempts to use different types of sentences, but in doing so creates an uneven flow rather than a smooth, seamless one.

Some of the sentences are stringy and awkward. "They were hiding from the Gestapo, an elite branch of the German police, specifically issued to capture and bring in the Jewish race and those affiliated with them" rolls smoothly. "Anne however in the midst of all this war and confusion, was still a teenage girl, and her feelings and emotions left behind only in her diary tell a story of a perfectly ordinary girl, turned extraordinary, by certain circumstances and her famous diary" does not.

C. Capturing Smooth and Rhythmic Flow

The writer has produced a text that is uneven. Many sentences read smoothly, while others are choppy or awkward.

Sentences such as "She liked hanging out with Peter and started to really like him and have a strong relationship with him in the later stages of their acquaintance" cry out for revision.

D. Breaking the "Rules" to Create Fluency

The writer diverges from standard English to create interest and impact. For example, he or she may use a sentence fragment, such as "All alone in the forest," or a single word, such as "Bam!" to accent a particular moment or action. He or she might begin with informal words such as *well, and,* or *but* to create a conversational tone, or he or she might break rules intentionally to make dialogue sound authentic.

The writer bends standard sentence convention by using second person in "You can't get much more normal than that" and by beginning a sentence with "and." These choices help develop an authentic voice.

What We Say to the Writer

The way you committed yourself to this idea and used information effectively make this piece enjoyable to read. Most of your sentences work well, but there are several places where they need revision. It's your job to make the information accessible to the reader in well-constructed sentences so they don't have to work so hard to understand. Your ideas should jump off the page; this can't happen if the reader is rereading parts to figure out where the sentences start and stop. Start by reading your piece out loud, paying strict attention to the punctuation you have on the paper. When you stop, pause, or have to back up, you will be able to hear the parts that need revising.

Scoring Guide

The paper rated these scores on a 6-point scale.

Ideas	5
Organization	4
Voice	4
Word Choice	5
SENTENCE FLUENCY	**4**
Conventions	5

"Have you heard of Anne Frank?"

Have you heard of Anne Frank? In the last fifty years her story has been made popular throughout the world. In World War Two, Anne Frank, a Jewish German, went into hiding with her parents, sister, another family, and a single man. They were hiding from the Gestapo, an elite branch of the German police, specifically issued to capture and bring in the Jewish race and those affiliated with them. Anne however in the midst of all this war and confusion, was still a teenage girl, and her feelings and emotions left behind only in her diary tell the story of a perfectly ordinary girl, turned extraordinary, by certain circumstances and her famous diary.

Anne used her leisure time like any other teen in her time or ours. She put pictures of movie stars on her wall, liked hanging out with her friends and was really outgoing. In the play "Anne Frank" she says that she was going to play ping-pong with her friend the afternoon she went into hiding. You can't get much more normal than that. She liked hanging out with Peter and started to really like him and have a strong relationship with him in the later stages of their acquaintance. She was kind of flirty with other people and just had fun in life. She took pleasure in being outdoors and loved her family. Anne was the normal, German, young teen.

Another way that Anne wasn't too different from the rest of us was very outspoken and opinionated. Every time she got into a controversial conversation, she automatically told it like it was, (in her opinion). Even if the conversation didn't concern her at all she could find some way of weaseling herself into it by making random connections to herself about the subject. When Ann had serious conversations with her father or Peter she was brutally honest and just talked it out. People like you and me need the same thing when we feel strongly about something; jut saying it all helps us get it out of our systems and it lets us relax a little. With Anne it was no different.

A final way that Anne was like us was that she had her issues, just like we all do. She had a rocky relationship with her mother who Anne claimed "didn't understand her." She was under a lot of pressure to be perfect and not do anything that would jeopardize the very lives of the people she knew and loved (and some that she didn't love). The whole government was out to get her and those like her. She was still in school and studying math, science and other subjects, but without the school building or any variety in teachers. Also, she was constantly being compared to her sister Margot, and had a big grudge against, not necessarily her sister, but those who compared her to Margot.

Anne Frank went through a lot in her lifetime and it really took its toll on her. Her life was cut short by an evil man's plan to wipe out a race She left behind a fist hand account of her time in hiding that the world would grow to know and love. Still, she was a human being. Not a hero because she was powerful, or strong, or smart, or talented, but because she was normal. She's unique, yet, just like everyone else. And that's what makes it special, what makes everything special. The sheer irony or being special is that it's so entirely and utterly normal. That's Anne Frank.

Analysis of the Sentence Fluency Trait in "'To the editor' (energy)"

What We See in the Writing

The ideas and the sentences in this piece are not working as well together as they might. Awkward sentence constructions distract the reader. Sometimes the sentences are structured correctly but not punctuated, throwing the reader for a loop. The writer has basic sentence sense, but now he or she needs to put it into practice to support the ideas and create rhythm and flow. **Sentence Fluency Score: 3, Developing**

A. Crafting Well-Built Sentences

The writer offers simple sentences that are sound, but no long, complex sentences. He or she attempts to vary the beginnings and lengths of sentences.

Although the writer begins with choppy, simple sentences, by the third paragraph, he or she begins to add some complex structures. Many sentences begin with the word "Missouri," which is boring for the reader.

B. Varying Sentence Types

The writer exhibits basic sentence sense and offers some sentence variety. He or she attempts to use different types of sentences, but, in doing so, the writer creates an uneven flow rather than a smooth, seamless one.

The majority of sentences are fairly basic. Some sentences are awkwardly paired, such as "In Missouri we have many rivers and lakes which could be used for hydro electricity" planted next to "Yet the Missouri river is not dammed in Missouri, there are five major dams along the Mississippi river."

> ### Scoring Guide
> *The paper rated these scores on a 6-point scale.*
>
> | | |
> |---|---|
> | Ideas | 5 |
> | Organization | 4 |
> | Voice | 5 |
> | Word Choice | 4 |
> | **SENTENCE FLUENCY** | **3** |
> | Conventions | 5 |

C. Capturing Smooth and Rhythmic Flow

The writer has produced a text that is uneven. Many sentences read smoothly, while others are choppy or awkward.

Segments such as "Because the wind blows strongest at night when the need for electricity is low, the excess electricity can be used in hydrogen production" followed by "This hydrogen can then be used to power fuel cells" show us this writer has a feel for fluency. Unfortunately, other parts, such as the second paragraph, show the writer is struggling for control.

D. Breaking the "Rules" to Create Fluency

The writer includes fragments, but they seem more accidental than intentional. He or she uses informal words, such as *well, and,* and *but,* inappropriately to start sentences, and pays little attention to making dialogue sound authentic.

This writer does not appear to break rules intentionally. Because the piece does not have strong sentences, it's difficult to credit the writer with knowing how to interject fragments.

What We Say to the Writer

You are developing a sense of fluency: to move it along, keep reading! Do you have a favorite author? Pay attention to the writer's use of sentence structures in each book or article. To revise this piece, take some time to look at every single sentence, both individually and in relation to the surrounding sentences. Which sentence do you think is the strongest? Which is the most problematic? What is the difference between them? Can you rework your least favorites to create a sense of rhythm similar to the smooth sentences and passages? This might be a good activity to do with a peer who is having a similar problem.

"'To the editor' (energy)"

To the editor,

Missouri needs to be energy independent. We have many alternative sources of energy, such as: bio-diesel fuel, wind energy, and hydro electricity.

Missouri is an excellent position to produce bio diesel fuel. In Missouri there are three major companies producing bio diesel fuel. Bio diesel is a totally renewable fuel source. It is also clean burning, non toxic and bio degradable. This alternative fuel source gives an additional market for Missouri farmers to sell their excess crops.

Northwest Missouri hosts many wind turbines. These are used to produce electricity. The town of Rock Port, Missouri is the first town in America to be produce enough wind energy to meet 100% of the town's needs. Wind is very versatile. It can be used for several purposes such as pumping water, heating water, generating electricity. Because the wind blows strongest at night when the need for electricity is low, the excess electricity can be used in hydrogen production. This hydrogen can then be used to power fuel cells. This electricity can be used later when the demand is greater. Farmers and ranchers can also use small wind turbines to pump water for their livestock.

In Missouri we have many rivers and lakes which could be used for hydro electricity. Yet the Missouri river is not dammed in Missouri, there are five major dams along the Mississippi river. Those five dams produce an estimated 889,000 megawatt hours (mwh) per year. If we could capture half of that energy, it would be three times as much energy as we used in Missouri in all of 2004, which was 123,000 mwh. Missouri has the potential hydro-electric energy, now we need the power plants to harness it Also the only environmental problem would be to a few fish which would get sucked into the turbines.

With all these energy sources there is little to no reason we should need imported oil. We have all the energy sources we need. What we need now is the dedication and determination to use them.

Ideas

Organization

Voice

Word Choice

Sentence Fluency

Conventions

Analysis of the Sentence Fluency Trait in "Cinderella"

What We See in the Writing

Many sentences in this piece are short, simple, and stiff. It reads like a list rather than a composition. The piece feels like abrupt, staccato notes. It's awkward to read aloud, and although many of the sentences are correct, they are not fluent. **Sentence Fluency Score: 2, Emerging**

A. Crafting Well-Built Sentences

The writer's sentences, even simple ones, are often flawed. Sentence beginnings are repetitive and uninspired.

This writer does not begin every sentence with the same word or phrase, nor does he or she run sentences together. However, he or she makes few attempts to vary sentence structures, and several sentences are devoid of information, making them unnecessary. For example, the sentence "Although these stories are somewhat similar, they also have some differences" only states the obvious.

B. Varying Sentence Types

The writer uses a single, repetitive sentence pattern throughout or connects sentence parts with an endless string of transition words such as *and, but, or,* and *because*, which distracts the reader.

The sentences in this piece follow one basic pattern. The writer does not use the sentences to create variety, interest, or flow, so the reader is not artfully drawn into the writing.

C. Capturing Smooth and Rhythmic Flow

The writer has created a text that is a challenge to read aloud since the sentences are incomplete, choppy, stilted, rambling, and/or awkward.

It's easy to hear what this paper lacks when we read it aloud. It's hard to find a smooth pace or tempo as we read "The two stories also contain magic. Yeh-Shen had a magical fish. Algonquin married into a magical family."

D. Breaking the "Rules" to Create Fluency

The writer offers few or no simple, well-built sentences, making it impossible to determine whether he or she has done anything out of the ordinary. Global revision is necessary before sentences can be revised for stylistic and creative purposes.

Fragments contribute to the disjointed feeling of the piece. Readers must pause to make sure they haven't missed information at the beginning of each paragraph.

> ## Scoring Guide
> *The paper rated these scores on a 6-point scale.*
>
> | | |
> |---|---|
> | Ideas | 2 |
> | Organization | 2 |
> | Voice | 2 |
> | Word Choice | 2 |
> | **SENTENCE FLUENCY** | **2** |
> | Conventions | 2 |

What We Say to the Writer

Most of your sentences are complete thoughts, and that's where fluency begins. Let's find and fix the sentences that are incomplete. Now let's find a fluent passage in one of your favorite books or magazines. Focus on one paragraph you think reads smoothly. Mark the sentence types you find, using a different colored pencil for each. For example, you could underline all of the simple sentences with green, all of the compound sentences with blue, and so on. You will be amazed at the rainbow of colors you will see when you are finished. Then we will work on making your piece into a rainbow of sentences, too. One step at a time, though.

Cinderella

In the two Cinderella stories one is *The Algonquin Cinderella* by: Idreis Shah. These stories are both like a Cinderella story The other story is called *A Chinese Cinderella Story* by: Ling Louis. There problem is the both get mistreated.

The similarities between the stories are. One similarity is that the main characters are married. Yeh-Shen married a king and, the Algonquin Cinderella married the Invisible One. The two stories also contain magic. Yeh-Shen had a magical fish. Algonquin married into a magical family. Finally, the settings of the story are somewhat similar. Both characters come from small villages. Yeh-Shen lives in a caveillage in Southern China. Algonquin lives in a wig-wam in Canada. Although these stories are somewhat similar, they also have some differences.

The differences between the stories are. The main characters have different family structures. Yeh-Shen was an orphan. Algonquin lived with her father and two sisters. They both have different homes. Yeh-Shen lives in a wig-whom. Algonquin lives in a cave. They both get mistreated, differently. Algonquin Cinderella is thrown into a fire place. Yeh-She gets yelled at a lot.

They have always gotten mistreated for a long time. Sometimes they are not getting mistreated. I wonder how it is having an Invisible Husband. It is probably wonderful marring a king.

Analysis of the Sentence Fluency Trait in "'To the editor' (lunch and recess)"

What We See in the Writing

Reading this piece aloud is challenging because the writer breaks thoughts with little regard to conventions; many sentences begin and end in awkward places. Another challenge is that the sentence ideas are sometimes unconnected, so it's hard to follow this writer's thinking. To make this piece flow, the writer needs to work on the sound of the words as they form sentences. He or she can make reading easier by constructing correct sentences, too, even if they are only simple ones at first.

Sentence Fluency Score: 1, Rudimentary

A. Crafting Well-Built Sentences

The writer's sentences, even simple ones, are often flawed. Sentence beginnings are repetitive and uninspired.

Scanning the piece quickly from beginning to end, it's easy to spot repetitive sentence beginnings. The sentences are choppy, and sometimes they don't work at all.

B. Varying Sentence Types

The writer uses a single, repetitive sentence pattern throughout or connects sentence parts with an endless string of transition words such as *and, but, or,* and *because*, which distracts the reader.

The writer attempts to use complex sentences. However, most are not punctuated correctly. It is hard for the reader to make sense of several segments.

C. Capturing Smooth and Rhythmic Flow

The writer has created a text that is a challenge to read aloud since the sentences are incomplete, choppy, stilted, rambling, and/or awkward.

Readers will struggle to read this piece aloud. It's hard to know where to pause because the sentences don't always end in a logical place. This creates an unsteady gait for expressive reading.

D. Breaking the "Rules" to Create Fluency

The writer offers few or no simple, well-built sentences, making it impossible to determine whether he or she has done anything out of the ordinary. Global revision is necessary before sentences can be revised for stylistic and creative purposes.

This writer must work on clarity and correctness before he or she focuses on flow.

> ## Scoring Guide
>
> *The paper rated these scores on a 6-point scale.*
>
> Ideas 1
> Organization 2
> Voice 2
> Word Choice 1
> **SENTENCE FLUENCY** **1**
> Conventions 2

What We Say to the Writer

You've chosen a great topic to write to the editor about, but your sentences aren't working to communicate your ideas clearly. Sometimes traits work together to make a piece stronger, and I think in this case we should tackle your ideas right along with your sentences. Read this piece to me, and I will jot down any questions I have. We can talk about them, and you can make notes about information you might add to the next draft. Then read it to me again, and this time make note of where you pause and if the sentence on the page is punctuated to match your oral reading. Put a little check mark any place where you think a sentence is not working well. We'll go back over those places as you add in the new information.

"To the editor" (lunch and recess)

To the editor: Kids should get one hour for lunch and recess. So they can stay fit and won't have to eat really fast.

If you eat really fast then sometimes you get stomachaches. Its sometimes hard to think if your stomach hurts. Its bad for your body. Sometimes you still don't have enough time to eat all of your food.

If we have recess we will stay fit More and More people each day are getting bigger. Lots of people eat junk food. We will get exercise.

And don't you want your students to be happy?

Analysis of the Conventions Trait in "A Swish, a Swat, and a Thump"

What We See in the Writing

This writer provides the reader with all of the road signs needed to navigate through the piece. Spelling, even on trickier words, is correct, and the writer has taken risks with punctuation and come through with flying colors. There are no problems in grammar and usage, and the paragraphing is flawless. Capitalization skills are strong as well.
Conventions Score: 6, Exceptional

A. Checking Spelling

The writer spells sight words, high-frequency words, and less familiar words correctly. When he or she spells less familiar words incorrectly, those words are phonetically correct. Overall, the piece demonstrates control in spelling.

This writer not only spells most conventional words correctly, but also uses spelling to create authentic sounds. EEHOO is not a word spell-check will okay, but it certainly is something we might yell in this situation!

B. Punctuating Effectively and Paragraphing Accurately

The writer handles basic punctuation skillfully. He or she understands how to use periods, commas, question marks, and exclamation points to enhance clarity and meaning. Paragraphs are indented in the right places. The piece is ready for a general audience.

Reading this piece aloud is a delight; it's an artful combination of fluent sentences and stellar conventions. The writer gives the readers all of the right cues for a dramatic reading.

> ### Scoring Guide
> *The paper rated these scores on a 6-point scale.*
>
> Ideas 4
> Organization 4
> Voice 5
> Word Choice 5
> Sentence Fluency 4
> **CONVENTIONS** **6**

C. Capitalizing Correctly

The writer uses capital letters consistently and accurately. A deep understanding of how to capitalize dialogue, abbreviations, proper names, and titles is evident.

The writer throws in some unconventional capitalization to provide emphasis. The reader knows how to read the piece just as the writer intends.

D. Applying Grammar and Usage

The writer forms grammatically correct phrases and sentences. He or she shows care in applying the rules of standard English. The writer may break from those rules for stylistic reasons, but otherwise abides by them.

This writer has a good command of grammar, probably from reading a great deal. The writer even avoids mistakes many adults make, such as knowing when to use its *and not* it's.

What We Say to the Writer

Thanks for thinking carefully about spelling, punctuation, and grammar. You gave me clear directions through your use of conventions, especially when you used just the right word or let us know which words you wanted emphasized. I would suggest spending time tightening your ideas and checking to make sure your details are clear and strong, but as you do, keep up the good work with conventions.

A Swish, a Swat, and a Thump

"Ladies and gentlemen, please welcome your Arrowheads! Your starting point guard, Brent the Brick!"

Everyone leaps up and screams as the rest of the team is introduced. My mom is a very caring woman who just wants to see her oldest son play ball. She gets just as embarrassed as I do when my dad starts shouting. I'll get to him later. Anyway, my mother exclaims, "Ooo, Brent the Brick."

My brother is a great basketball player. He is always focused and loves to score. Oh yeah, I forgot to mention that he loves to feel tall. We yelled, "GO, BRENT!"

I'm sitting back and scouting the Timberwolves. I've never seen them play before, so I was very interested in how they play. I knew that my dad was just waiting to get mad at the Arrowheads and their mistakes. He takes the game more seriously than the players do! His face always turns red and so do his eyes. The players are warming up, just waiting to have their way with one another.

Soon the buzzer sounds and all of the pumped up fans are waiting for the jump ball. Everything is at a stand still. The ball is in the air. Then, the players soar into the air as if they have wings. Finally, the Timberwolves snag the ball away. Both teams go on a scoring run through the whole game, always keeping the score close. Each team's fans started to cheer louder and louder with every shot with a 'swish.' Then, it became personal.

I kept my eyes on the game, but I was hearing things that people were saying. I was hearing about fights, vandalism, etc. Then, a Timberwolves boy came up for a lay up. Brent came up right behind him and SWAT! It was all ball, but they called a foul. The fans went crazy! We were shouting our lungs out, "OHH, GET THAT STUFF OUT!"

It was awesome. The Arrowheads came tough. The thump of the basketball echoed throughout the gym. The swish rang through my ears and rattled my brain. The Arrowheads started to work together. They sunk shots. They, they . . . they WON!

I shouted, "EEHOOO!"

My dad's red colored face started to return to its normal color. As we were waiting for Brent to come out of the locker room, I looked back on the game. I remember saying in my head, "Guys, most of you have short tempers. Don't lose them tonight. Don't start something if you can't take the consequences!"

Analysis of the Conventions Trait in "'Six pairs of shoes'"

What We See in the Writing

This student is obviously an accomplished writer, yet he or she has problems with spelling simple words such as *sauce*. While some students are able to resolve this issue by memorizing words, applying spelling rules, and using resources, others struggle with spelling well into adulthood. Other conventions in the piece are very strong. The spelling is not problematic, but rather a relative weakness compared to the other conventions.
Conventions Score: 5, Strong

A. Checking Spelling

The writer spells sight words, high-frequency words, and less familiar words correctly. When he or she spells less familiar words incorrectly, those words are phonetically correct. Overall, the piece demonstrates control in spelling.

Although most words are correct, this writer slips up on some common words. Luckily, the piece is compelling and enjoyable, so we hardly notice the misspellings.

B. Punctuating Effectively and Paragraphing Accurately

The writer handles basic punctuation skillfully. He or she understands how to use periods, commas, question marks, and exclamation points to enhance clarity and meaning. Paragraphs are indented in the right places. The piece is ready for a general audience.

The writer uses punctuation quite effectively to guide the reader. Perhaps the writer gets a little carried away when using an exclamation point and a question mark, but it creates emphasis, and that was probably the intent. The story unfolds as the writer intended, with few stumbles in punctuation along the way.

C. Capitalizing Correctly

The writer uses capital letters consistently and accurately. A deep understanding of how to capitalize dialogue, abbreviations, proper names, and titles is evident.

Capitalization is under control. The writer uses capitalization as an extension of punctuation.

D. Applying Grammar and Usage

The writer forms grammatically correct phrases and sentences. He or she shows care in applying the rules of standard English. The writer may break from those rules for stylistic reasons, but otherwise abides by them.

Even when the writer breaks the rules, such as with "Want a sibling?" or "And I can tell you, it's not easy," it works. Even so, the writer struggles with a few common mistakes, such as writing your *when she means* you're.

> ## Scoring Guide
>
> *The paper rated these scores on a 6-point scale.*
>
> Ideas 6
>
> Organization 6
>
> Voice 6
>
> Word Choice 6
>
> Sentence Fluency 6
>
> **CONVENTIONS** **5**

What We Say to the Writer

Oh, that spelling demon! You know that spelling correctly is a completely different skill from knowing how to use ideas in writing, right? There are things you can do to help yourself with spelling. You might want to try keeping a list of problem words in your writer's notebook so you will know which words frequently elude you. Once you have determined a few, start tuning in to those words as you read and write, purposefully lingering on them until the correct spelling or usage imprints itself on your mind. Just work on one or two at a time, but don't strike them off your list once you've worked on them. You will need to revisit the list often. And in the meantime, nice work on the other conventions and all the other traits!

"Six pairs of shoes"

Six pairs of shoes are in a muddy pile, the smell of tomato sause wafts in from the kitchen. Foot steps thunk loudly above you, and you can hear music from a guitar piano, and drum, all battaling to burst your ear drum. In addition you can hear an occasional "Oh my gosh!' echoing from the dining room, as my sister carries on a "life or death" phone call. Now look to your left, there's me trying to read in the midst of all the chaos. Want a sibling? I've got six!

At the beginning of my life I was a normal kid, a mom, dad, big sister and little brother. Then my parents got divorced, now add two stepparents, three stepbrothers, and one stepsister. In addition to three dogs, five cats, ten fish, and two lizards. If you ever want peace, quite, or alone time, do not join my family!

Right now some of you are probably asking how I live in the midst of people yelling, "Hey, that's mine," "It's my turn!", "OMG! Sandy's going out with him?!" and "Can SOMEONE please let out the dog!" And I can tell you, its not easy. But now picture having a sports wiz, a 4.26 GPA student, an artist, a business student, and a want-to-be WMBA player to go to for advice, and having all those people there to comfort you when your down.

My siblings are like my arms and legs. Do I take them for granted? Yes. Do I want to have them taken away? No! I've had them for so long that I could never imagine life without them. I love being able to go home, knowing that someone will ask how my day went or about how I did on my big test.

Asking me to be an only child would be like cutting away 3/4ths of my heart. I know that may seem a little dramatic, and sure my brothers and sisters get annoying but if you saw how kind and caring my siblings are, then you would understand why I would rather have brothers and sisters than be an only child.

Analysis of the Conventions Trait in "'We're not supposed to'"

What We See in the Writing

This writer punctuates most of the dialogue correctly, but the number of minor mistakes indicates a lack of polish in the editing stage, in which the writer gets the piece ready for the reader. It appears that the writer didn't bother using spell-check, because that would have caught several of the mistakes. Using readily available resources can be a big help in conventions. **Conventions Score: 4, Refining**

A. Checking Spelling

The writer incorrectly spells a few high-frequency words and many unfamiliar words and/or sophisticated words.

The writer spells words like specifically *and* panicked *correctly, yet he misspells* not *and* in. *The writer needs to run though his draft twice during the editing stage—once for spelling only and once for the other conventions.*

B. Punctuating Effectively and Paragraphing Accurately

The writer handles basic punctuation marks (such as end marks on sentences and commas in a series) well. However, he or she might have trouble with more complex punctuation marks (such as quotation marks, parentheses, dashes) and with paragraphing, especially on longer pieces.

The writer is inconsistent. He correctly punctuates much of the dialogue, but he leaves out a period here and a comma there. He also throws in some run-on sentences, which force the reader to reread for comprehension.

> ### Scoring Guide
> *The paper rated these scores on a 6-point scale.*
>
> Ideas 4
> Organization 5
> Voice 4
> Word Choice 3
> Sentence Fluency 3
> **CONVENTIONS** **4**

C. Capitalizing Correctly

The writer capitalizes the first word in sentences and most common proper names. However, his or her use of more complex capitalization is spotty within dialogue, abbreviations, and proper names (*Aunt Maria* versus *my aunt*, for instance).

The writer seems to have a better understanding of capitalization than punctuation. Most of the mistakes he makes with capitalization are connected to punctuation problems.

D. Applying Grammar and Usage

The writer has made grammar and usage mistakes throughout the piece, but they do not interfere with the reader's ability to understand the message. Issues related to agreement, tense, and word usage appear here and there, but can be easily corrected.

The writer seems to have a good sense of grammar and usage, except when his punctuation is off. Even his usage problem with were *versus* we're *is connected to a punctuation error.*

What We Say to the Writer

I like your confidence in using dialogue. Just remember, you must review your writing very carefully to ensure that you have given the reader all of the guidance you can with conventions. While your efforts are evident, the remaining mistakes indicate a need for more careful editing. Slow down, read the piece aloud exactly as you wrote it, and note the places where you skipped letters or punctuation marks. If you use contractions, go back and say the full phrase, instead of the contraction, to make sure you have the right version on the paper. For example, if you'd said "we are" in the phrase "who we're found the next morning," I'm sure you would have realized the mistake. Then ask a peer to look through it with you. It is usually easier for someone else to catch our editing mistakes.

"We're not supposed to"

"We're not supposed to be back here," Charlie reminded his brother and his brother's friend, Matthew.

"So?" Kevin asked, "Mom's not home, so if we get back in time mom won't find out." Charlie agreed but it didn't make him feel any better about going into the woods that his mother specifically told him to stay away from. They walked for about forty-five minutes before Kevin decided to go back home.

"This is borring," Kevin said "theres nothing back here so lets just go back." Charlie was relieved to hear his brother say this.

"Which way did we come from?" Matthew asked.

"It was this way, I'm sure," Kevin lied to prevent Matthew and Charlie from knowing, they could be lost. They walked on for about an hour, when Charlie finally realized that they couldn't be going the right way.

"Hey," Charlie said. "We've been walking for a long time and we're still no back yet." That's when Charlie panicked, he ran n circles trying to find a way to get out he eventualy tripped on a root and fell to the ground. He looked down and realized he had cut his leg open. It wasn't bad, but at the first sign of blood, Matthew passed out. Charlie and Kevin starred down at Matthew, trying to think of what to do about there new problem.

"We could try to carry or pull him with us," Charlie suggested. They looked down at him and remembered that he was about fifty pounds overweight, so even pulling him wasnt an option. They decided to leave him there and come back when they got some help. They walked even farther until they met up with a bear.

"Just stay still and don't make any noises and it will leave us alone." Kevin told Charlie. But Charlie didn't listen he just ran away screaming like a maniac. The bear didn't bother chasing them though it just walked in the opposite direction. Charlie realized that he had made a stupid decision and was now alone. So he tried his own method of being lost and stayed in the same spot.

Meanwhile, instead of staying in the same spot, Kevin had a flashlight and was still looking for a way out. After about fifteen minutes he found a trail and followed it to a house. He knocked on the door and a surprised old man answered it. He let Kevin use his phone to call his parents, who came and picked him up. They set out a serch party for Matthew and Charlie, who we're found the next morning. The three of them were grounded for two years.

Analysis of the Conventions Trait in "Kalahari"

What We See in the Writing

The writer is inconsistent in the use of conventions, and needs to spend time editing the piece before sharing it with a reader. For writers, it's easy to read what was intended rather than what was written, so working with a partner would aid this writer's editing process. **Conventions Score: 3, Developing**

A. Checking Spelling

The writer incorrectly spells a few high-frequency words and many unfamiliar words and/or sophisticated words.

The writer spells words correctly—great. Along with this good spelling, the reader will appreciate time spent on the other conventions.

B. Punctuating Effectively and Paragraphing Accurately

The writer handles basic punctuation marks (such as end marks on sentences and commas in a series) well. However, he or she might have trouble with more complex punctuation marks (such as quotation marks, parentheses, dashes) and with paragraphing, especially on longer pieces.

In several places, the writer's lack of correct punctuation causes the reader to stop and sort out the text. Sentences such as "First off we went to the slides they were great but the best part was going on it with my grandparents I went down every slide I could with them and the ones I couldn't they were at the bottom to great me" stretch the definition of a run-on!

> ### Scoring Guide
> *The paper rated these scores on a 6-point scale.*
>
> | | |
> |---|---|
> | Ideas | 3 |
> | Organization | 4 |
> | Voice | 4 |
> | Word Choice | 3 |
> | Sentence Fluency | 3 |
> | **CONVENTIONS** | **3** |

C. Capitalizing Correctly

The writer capitalizes the first word in sentences and most common proper names. However, his or her use of more complex capitalization is spotty within dialogue, abbreviations, and proper names (*Aunt Maria* versus *my aunt*, for instance).

The writer shows some inconsistency by capitalizing Wisconsin *but not* Dells. *He also randomly capitalizes some words in the middle of the sentence "We Moved on to one of my favorite past times, Being lazy."*

D. Applying Grammar and Usage

The writer has made grammar and usage mistakes throughout the piece, but they do not interfere with the reader's ability to understand the message. Issues related to agreement, tense, and word usage appear here and there, but can be easily corrected.

Pronouns confuse this writer. There are problems with you, and the writer does not understand when to use subjective versus objective pronouns. An example of this confusion is found in the sentence "One of the best times I had was when my grandma forced her and I to go down the slide called the master blaster."

What We Say to the Writer

It's sometimes helpful to isolate one convention at a time as you edit. Your spelling is terrific, so that's one down. I think we need to spend some time reviewing pronouns. I can tell you are struggling with them. Once we do that, review all the pronouns in your piece to check them. Next, work on breaking your thoughts into sentences by using punctuation marks. As you read, note where natural pauses occur. Trade papers with some of your classmates to see how they handled conventions and to get their feedback. Be patient with yourself; it takes time to master conventions.

Kalahari

Water rushing and swooshing all around you as you go faster, faster and faster. Until you come out of the dark tunnel unharmed and untouched with and exhilarated look upon your face as you're greeted by grandparents into America's largest indoor pool in the Wisconsin dells. This trip was some of the best fun I've ever had and there was a lot to be had. This could have been from all the water slides the raft slides me and my grandparents went on.

First off we went to the slides they were great but the best part was going on it with my grandparents I went down every slide I could with them and the ones I couldn't they were at the bottom to greet me. I went down one of my favorite slides where you can go up to 40 mph, around a funnel, on at least six times and they were always there. One of the best times I had was when my grandma forced her and I to go down the slide called the master blaster. This slide goes up and down it was like a roller coaster, there were super strong water jets that shoot your raft up the slopes; it was so much fun we went on it multiple times.

We Moved on to one of my favorite past times, Being lazy. The lazy river was fantastic the whole time we were in the lazy river my family and I pushed each other into the multitude of waterfalls and water jets. One time I even flipped my grandpa's inner tube and he's 60!

Sadly the trip ended but this was one of the best times I've ever had and I'll remember it. But what really set it apart was the fact that my grandparents who are from a small town would go to a big town and even go into the water like they did. I'm really glad got to go there with them.

Analysis of the Conventions Trait in "'My Grandpa'"

What We See in the Writing

This piece clearly shows how important the conventions trait really is. The numerous errors, especially in spelling, make the reading a real challenge. That frustration could make readers miss the poignant story hidden beneath all of the problems. When writers have something important to say, it's the right time to work on conventions because they will want others to read and enjoy their writing, too.

Conventions Score: 2, Emerging

A. Checking Spelling

The writer has misspelled many words, even simple ones, which causes the reader to focus on conventions rather than on the central theme or storyline.

Spelling problems are abundant. This writer has trouble with both simple and complex words. Some examples include ther *for* there, blak *for* black, supper stition *for* superstition, *and* colon *for* cologne.

B. Punctuating Effectively and Punctuating Accurately

The writer has neglected to use punctuation, used punctuation incorrectly, and/or forgotten to indent paragraphs, making it difficult for the reader to find meaning.

The paragraphing is fine, and the writer uses complete sentences most of the time. The punctuation is not 100 percent, but the writer shows a good understanding of how to use it effectively.

> ## Scoring Guide
>
> *The paper rated these scores on a 6-point scale.*
>
> Ideas 4
>
> Organization 3
>
> Voice 4
>
> Word Choice 3
>
> Sentence Fluency 3
>
> **CONVENTIONS** **2**

C. Capitalizing Correctly

The writer uses capitals inconsistently, even in common places such as the first word in the sentence. He or she uses capitals correctly in some places, but has no consistent control over them.

The writer shows inconsistency with capitalization, missing capitalization on some of the sentence starts and capitalizing grandpa *when it should not be.*

D. Applying Grammar and Usage

The writer makes frequent mistakes in grammar and usage, making it difficult to read and understand the piece. Issues related to agreement, tense, and word usage abound.

This writer struggles with word usage, as evidenced by the use of here *for* hear *and* talks *for* says. *There is also some stumbling over verb tense, which causes some confusion, since present-tense verbs in the last paragraph make it sound as though the grandfather is alive.*

What We Say to the Writer

What a great tribute to your grandfather! I hope you polish this piece and then share it with your family. Since spelling is the biggest editing issue in this piece, I would suggest typing this and using spell-check to help. But that won't solve all of your spelling problems. You need to think about what is causing you problems and look for patterns so you can address them. For example, did you misspell *black* because you don't know how to spell it or because you didn't edit your draft? Once you have determined this, we will be able to create an editing goal for your next draft.

"My Grandpa"

My Grandpa (or papo that means Grandpa) died when I was born. I haven't ever seen his face well exept in picturs and I here about him alot. It's not fun when he's not ther, papo (pa-po) my Grandpa met me but I didn't ever meet him. It hurts me because I don't have one Grandpa. Not one, both of them died.

Papo had brown blak hair, and blue eyes. He is very tall also he's realy thin. He's about '5" 10". He's very supper stition. (You will here more about that latter). Grandpa dressed rich. With a tie and fancy shoes, (He was a post man) only when he wasnt on post. Colon was what made him smell rich. It smelled like peprmint.

My papo was very supper station. if tell a girl she's beautiful he woul right away say somethig eles about her so the devle wont take her beauty away. My Grandpa would alway make you lagh so hard you would fall off your feet. At least thats what I heard. He loved me so much is what evry boady told me.

I rember by evryone telling me about him. Also because I have picturs of him. My family only talks good things about him. When I look at picturs of him I cry. I wish he was standing right next to me. He's nice "and" he's funny. He loves evry one. When someone would walk by he'd tell them how proud he is to be a greek. Now you can see why I wish he was here.

Analysis of the Conventions Trait in "Candan Dive Trip"

What We See in the Writing

Problems with conventions, especially the nonstandard spelling, create a puzzle for us to solve instead of a story to enjoy. Because the spelling is so problematic, the piece is very hard to read and would require extensive editing. This piece needs editing in all areas of conventions, though, before it is readable.
Conventions Score: 1, Rudimentary

A. Checking Spelling

The writer has misspelled many words, even simple ones, which causes the reader to focus on conventions rather than on the central theme or storyline.

This writer tries to tell a good story with lots of details, but egregious spelling errors are a real stumbling block. Reading and translating sentences such as "After he was doun etang, we swam to the bow of he vesal to collect poltion scalups" takes patience and skill.

B. Punctuating Effectively and Punctuating Accurately

The writer has neglected to use punctuation, used punctuation incorrectly, and/or forgotten to indent paragraphs, making it difficult for the reader to find meaning.

The writer punctuates some of the sentences correctly, but several are either separated incorrectly into multiple sentences or linked into long, run-on sentences. Punctuation is not seriously flawed like the spelling, but it is not under control.

> ### Scoring Guide
> *The paper rated these scores on a 6-point scale.*
>
> Ideas 3
> Organization 3
> Voice 3
> Word Choice 3
> Sentence Fluency 3
> **CONVENTIONS 1**

C. Capitalizing Correctly

The writer uses capitals inconsistently even in common places such as the first word in the sentence. He or she uses capitals correctly in some places, but has no consistent control over them.

Of the four key qualities, this is the one the writer seems to understand the best. Every time the writer ends a thought with a punctuation mark, he or she begins the next thought with a capital letter. Most proper nouns, as well as the pronoun I, are capitalized.

D. Applying Grammar and Usage

The writer makes frequent mistakes in grammar and usage, making it difficult to read and understand the piece. Issues related to agreement, tense, and word usage abound.

Because the words are so poorly spelled, it's hard to evaluate the writer's grammar and usage. There are a couple of obvious problems, such as using herd *for* heard *and misplacing the modifier "eating out of my hands."*

What We Say to the Writer

Your diving experience sounds amazing! You did a great job sticking to one idea and giving details to help us visualize your adventure. Unfortunately, I had a hard time figuring that out because of the spelling. You typed it, so let's explore how to use spell-checker to help! I am very impressed that you show such strong capitalization skills. There's a lot to think about when you edit writing, so let's begin with spelling and go on from there.

Candan Dive Trip

One year my family and I went to Canda for a dive trip by the powell river. One day we weant to a shipwreck it was a Candian destroyer. The only way to the wreck is by bout. When we go to our destination there were three bouts. One at bow, midship and one at stern.

We started to sut up. This is the part I hate. Because you have to put on a hot tight neoprene wetsute booties hood and gloves. Then putting on a seventy-five tank with an additional twent pounds of weight in my bouncey control devvese (B.C.D.) Because I have the weight intgrated B.C.D. That means the weight is put into BCD Instead of a weightbelt.

As I waited for everyone else to get suited up, I went in to the water using the rolover bakword method. When everyone was in the water they swame over to the anker line. I gave the desent signal. We all started our desent.

As I was desending in to the darknes, I turnd on my flashlight about sixty feet. I wasshing it on the bottom. When all of a soden I saw it. The Ship. I was about ninty feet when I landed on the six inch naval gun mounted on the deck.

My dad and I started to look around when I saw a seventy inch eel with a one foot in diameter head. His name is Captain crunch. He is a pet to every one who dives there. I saw a big bright purpal see erchon on the seabed so I dove down and got it. When I got back he was like a pupy dog bagin for food. So, I cut the urchin up and fed it to him. I was nervos because he is an anamal that is uppriditable and has the jaw presser of one thosand pound per sqwar inch, eating out of my hands. After he was doun etang, we swam to the bow of the vesal to collect poltion scalups, they were swimming around like buter flays.

I went to the helm to look arund when i got thir there were all the inster ments and controls were stell intact. The wood stering weel was thir too. After I stopt swimming around I landed on the flor and I desvord that under all the sut and seltment that there was a the wight and black checkerd flor, so I wrot my name on the flor. As I was living I herd a beping sound I locked at my dive computer and it was teling me tht I had to make my asent.

I sed "good by intell next time" to the ship. At thats how I decovered that I was a good diver.

Guidelines for Using the Interactive PDFs on the CD

On the enclosed CD, you'll find PDFs of all 36 papers from the book. You can print them or project them onto a screen for whole-class discussion, using your whiteboard tools to highlight, comment, and even revise and edit.

In addition, you'll find 12 interactive PDFs—a high and a low paper for each trait. Navigation buttons at the bottom of each page step you through the four key qualities for the particular trait. For each key quality, Think Abouts—questions that guide revision or editing—appear, as does a teacher comment that discusses how the key quality was handled in the paper. You'll also find a final page in each PDF on which students are prompted either to revise part of a low paper (indicated by the "Revise" navigation button) or to try out a revision strategy modeled in a high piece on their own writing (indicated by the "Try It" navigation button). Editing activities are provided for the conventions trait as well.

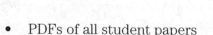

Here's a sample routine for working with the Interactive PDFs

1. Display the paper from the Interactive PDFs folder.

2. Read the paper as a class.

3. Review the corresponding scoring guide. You may display this side-by-side with the paper or have students consult their own copies.

4. Discuss the paper and arrive at a consensus score, based on the scoring guide. Record it on the line indicated.

5. Compare your score with our score; click on the "Score" button to reveal how we scored the paper.

6. Explore one or more key qualities by clicking on the corresponding navigation buttons at the bottom of the page. The highlighted parts indicate words or passages we focused on as we evaluated the paper. Scroll over the teacher comment icon to see our discussion of how the key quality was handled in the paper.

7. Offer revision practice by clicking on the "Revise" button for the low papers or the "Try It" button for the high papers. Have students follow the directions on that page to apply revision strategies.

> **TIP**
>
> To view and print the files on the CD, you need Adobe Reader™, version 7.0 or higher. You can download it free of charge for Mac and PC systems at http://www.adobe.com/products/acrobat

CD Contents

- Scoring Guides (teacher version)
- Student-Friendly Scoring Guides
- Editor's Marks reference sheet
- Think About (student sheets)

- PDFs of all student papers
- Guidelines for Using the Interactive PDFs on the CD
- 12 Interactive PDFs

We recommend that you view the interactive PDFs in full screen mode.

Using Benchmark Papers to Teach Writing With the Traits: Middle School © 2010 by Ruth Culham, Scholastic Teaching Resources